"Shze-Hui Tjoa's *The Story Game* is a beau[...]ing interrogation of memory, a memoir unlike any I've ever read. A powerful work of art and healing."

—JAQUIRA DÍAZ,
author of *Ordinary Girls*

"Shze-Hui Tjoa's *The Story Game* is a patient excavation of selves: not the I of today, but the version before and the one before that, flawed and flawing, all the way back to childhood, reaching through history and memory to dust free so many cruel reflections. Ardently exquisite, Shze-Hui Tjoa tenders astonishment with blushing tenacity."

—LILY HOÀNG,
author of *A Bestiary*

"Reading this, I forgot about the real room I was in. I felt fully contained in the invented room separating *The Story Game's* chapters. In The Room, Shze-Hui Tjoa makes make-believe serious the way children do—but she does it by playing with the memoir genre. As her storytelling progresses, she plunges, as the greatest writers have, to The Depths, revealing how the artistic process transforms her understanding of mind and body. Her ascent into The World is startling and powerful. After I read it, I felt a new world of creative possibilities opening. *The Story Game* is hyper-specific yet ethereal, serious and funny. It's mesmerizing."

—JEANNIE VANASCO,
author of *Things We Didn't Talk
About When I Was a Girl*

# THE STORY GAME

# THE
# STORY
# GAME

*a memoir*

SHZE-HUI
TJOA

TIN HOUSE / PORTLAND, OREGON

Copyright © 2024 by Shze-Hui Tjoa
First US Edition 2024
Printed in the United States of America

Epigraph credit: Edith Södergran, excerpt from "On Foot I Wandered Through the Solar Systems," translated by Malena Mörling and Jonas Ellerström, from *On Foot I Wandered Through the Solar Systems: Poems* (Marick Press, 2012). | Epigraph credit: Tomas Tranströmer, excerpt from "Vermeer," translated by Patty Crane, from *Bright Scythe: Selected Poems.* Copyright © 2015 by Tomas Tranströmer. English translation copyright © 2015 by Patty Crane. Reprinted with the permission of The Permissions Company, LLC on behalf of Sarabande Books, sarabandebooks.org. | Quoted lines from Clifford Geertz on p. 12 are used with permission of MIT Press Journals, from "Deep Play: Notes on the Balinese Cockfight (1972)," *Daedalus* 134, no. 4 (Fall 2005): 56–86. © 1972 by the American Academy of Arts and Sciences. | Quoted lines from Simone Weil on p. 70 and 74 are used with permission of Taylor & Francis Informa UK Ltd - Books, from *Gravity and Grace*, Simone Weil, translated by Emma Crawford and Mario von der Ruhr, 1st edition © 2002; permission conveyed through Copyright Clearance Center, Inc. | Quoted lines from Simone Weil on p. 71 are used with permission of Taylor & Francis Informa UK Ltd - Books, from *Waiting for God*, Simone Weil, 1st edition © 2021; permission conveyed through Copyright Clearance Center, Inc.

Manufacturing by Sheridan | Interior design by Beth Steidle

Library of Congress Cataloging-in-Publication Data

Names: Tjoa, Shze-Hui, 1993– author.
Title: The story game : a memoir / Shze-Hu Tjoa.
Description: Portland, Oregon : Tin House, [2024]
Identifiers: LCCN 2024000287 | ISBN 9781959030751 (paperback) |
ISBN 9781959030768 (ebook)
Subjects: LCSH: Tjoa, Shze-Hui, 1993– | Girls—Singapore—Biography. | East Asians—England—London—Biography. | Singapore—Biography. | London (England)—Biography. | Depression, Mental—Singapore. | Depression, Mental—England—London.
Classification: LCC DS610.73.T56 A3 2024 | DDC 959.57/053—dc23/eng/20240110
LC record available at https://lccn.loc.gov/2024000287

Tin House | 2617 NW Thurman Street, Portland, OR 97210 | www.tinhouse.com

DISTRIBUTED BY W. W. NORTON & COMPANY

1 2 3 4 5 6 7 8 9 0

*Dedicated to Thomas.*

*Thank you for everything.*

On foot
I wandered through the solar systems,
before I found the first thread of my red dress.
Already I have a sense of myself.

—EDITH SÖDERGRAN,
*translated by Malena Mörling*
*and Jonas Ellerström*


No sheltered world . . . Right behind the wall the noise begins
. . . . . . . . . . . . . . . . . . . . . . . . . . . . . .
It hurts to go through walls, and makes you sick
but it's necessary.
The world is one.

—TOMAS TRANSTRÖMER,
*translated by Patty Crane*

# CONTENTS

# THE STORY GAME

# PROLOGUE

You've forgotten so much, Hui. About the past. About yourself.

What was that game we used to play when we were children?
We played it every night, before things went wrong between us.
     It was a story game, wasn't it?

Wake up, Hui.

Let's play our game again, so that you remember.

# YEAR ONE

*The Room*

NIGHT-TIME IN THE ROOM AGAIN. ENDLESS NIGHT.
Stillness in the firmament and a hush across the seas. Outside
our windows, the moon tilts its face towards us, and a chorus
of cricket sounds rises and falls. The ceiling fan churns thick,
humid swashes of air above our heads: a slow tropical eddy,
scented by the eucalyptus oil burner that our mother has left
on for us.

What else is here with us, in the room? What items of
furniture; what sorts of pictures on the walls? It's hard for me
to say. I don't know how long we've been lying here—two
sisters sharing this mattress on the floor. Months now, or
maybe years? It's so very dark, Nin, but I know that you're
here with me. And when we're together like this, we can be
or do anything: live out our other lives, construct our secret
universes.

*Hui?* your voice says. It sounds the way I remember it from
a long time ago, with the pitch and tone of a little girl again.

*Hui, are you awake?*

*Can you tell me a story?*

# ROOM

Hui?

*. . . Hm?*

Are you awake?

*Well, I am now. Why?*

Can't sleep. I'm scared. Can you tell me a story?

. . . Please!

*Fine. What kind of story do you want?*

About somewhere magical and far away—you know! A
perfect place.

*Those don't exist.*

What?

*They don't exist, Nin. These places from our stories that you
think are perfect. Where magical oak trees touch the sky or
bazaars sell flying carpets.*

How about the jungle with talking animals? Whose eyes light up the night?

*The real-life place it's based on is disappointing, too.*

Really?

*Yes. You'll see.*

*If you ever get to visit it outside this room, like I have.*

I don't believe you, Hui!

*What? Why?*

You act like you know everything—just because I'm little in this room. But you're lying to me, right?

*What do you mean?*

I bet all the places from our stories are amazing!

*No! I swear—they're very ordinary. Broken, and full of problems.*

*Trust me, I'm so much older now.*

Why don't you prove it to me?

*How?*

Tell me a story about one of these places. Somewhere you've visited recently.

And make sure you use your grown-up voice when you're telling me the story.

*The voice with all the big words?*

Yeah—do you remember it? You've been asleep here for so long.

*I'm sure it'll come back to me.*

I'll guide you along the way.

Just make sure that it's a true story about your other life, outside this room. That's the most important thing, so I can feel close to you again.

*I'd like that too, Nin.*

*To feel close to you again.*

# HUI'S FIRST STORY

## The Island Paradise

### I

OCTOBER HAS COME to Bali, drenching it in sweat. The air hangs over us, weighted and still. The whole island is holding its breath, preparing for the atmosphere to dip—for the pendulum swing of the first monsoon rains.

The minivan driver has brought me to Seminyak Square—one of the busiest stretches on Bali's south coast—in search of a bookstore. "You want books for tourists?" he asks me, weaving deftly around the knots in traffic.

"No, no," I protest, suddenly self-conscious. I try to switch languages to prove my point: "*Sebenarnya pak*, I'm looking for books to improve my Bahasa."

"*Ya*," he responds, switching languages too. "So like I just said: books for tourists."

He drops me off by an air-conditioned boutique. Inside, the shelves mostly stock Lonely Planet guidebooks. Glossy coffee-table books line the display windows, their covers adorned with the usual themes: beaches, thatched roofs, dancing women.

The minivan will be back in twenty minutes. I pay for a guidebook, then wander outside. In the open-air car park, a band is setting up to busk: a keyboardist, a guitarist, and a singer. Another band member sits splay-legged across a *cajón*, anxiously shoveling the last of his lunch from an oily brown wrapper into his mouth.

The taxis and shoppers idle around them: three men and a woman in too-warm denim jackets. When the band is ready, the woman begins to sing. The piece is Alicia Keys's remake of "Empire State of Mind," an ode to New York City from 2010. It's popular here, eight years later, in Bali's tourist district, like so many other cultural icons that have long lapsed out of favor elsewhere—caramel Frappuccinos, or harem pants.

The singer's diction is immaculately studied, a one-to-one syllabic mirror of Keys. But her amp is old, dented, and rusty. On her tight black T-shirt, bejeweled lettering spells out the mock-English phrase "Princess Maybe Me." Has she set eyes on another country before? Or on New York City—that place of opportunity and big dreams she's singing so fervently about?

Some of the other tourists have stopped as well, forming a crowd of listeners around the band. There's an emotion in the woman's voice that makes it difficult to look away—wrenching the lyrics of the song apart with all the tautness and precarity of an open trap. She seems to have picked out some undertone in the ballad and swelled it full of force; there's something living in her voice, straining against the confines of chorus and verse.

A feeling leaps into being around us, hot and brash and sour. And then the song ends; the tourists clap. People reach for their wallets and shake their heads, as if coming out of a daze.

*I know what this is,* I tell myself. *This feeling of rancor in her voice.*
*What else were they expecting?*
*What else could it be?*

## II

BECAUSE I AM half-Indonesian on our father's side, I have
heard many stories about Bali before visiting for the first time.
Based on these stories, I assume that I am privy to a secret
pattern worked deep into the grain of the island's history.

Broadly speaking, this pattern has to do with power and
the variegated way that it falls upon the different people of
the earth. Specifically, it has to do with the people who live
on this island and the imbalances that define their relationship with everyone else.

A secondhand story, by way of explaining what I mean.

In the late 1950s—this particular story goes—an American
anthropologist named Clifford Geertz moves to Bali for
fieldwork. While observing the locals, he grows curious
about the cockfights that materialize every few days in the
village where he lives. What, he wonders, drives this strange
Balinese obsession with squatting in a circle, placing bets,
and watching armed fowl gouge each other to death?

After some consideration, Geertz arrives at a version of
the truth: that cockfighting is, really, an aesthetic form like
the theater. A good fight can take the ordinary concerns
of a village—men backing their cousins or betting against
rivals—and wring pure spectacle out of them. It can make the
everyday quiver with blood, fear, and animal guts—wrapping
it in the language of allegory and raising it to the level of art.

During each round, two cock owners place bets of matching amounts, followed by an onrush of side betting from spectators. The birds then clash briefly until a winner is announced. In that moment, change seems to overtake the village: paupers revel in newfound riches while landlords tumble from grace, ceding honor to those whom they usually command. Glory speeds helter-skelter through the village hierarchy, anointing new kings and dethroning the losers.

But there is another, more pertinent similarity between a cockfight and a piece of theater. Like a black box, the cockfight is a world set apart: all of its drama is self-contained, rarely crossing the threshold of the stage. Within each match, so much money can change hands that village hierarchies might seem to be shifting. But the reality is that these hierarchies are, ultimately, set in stone: the rules of the game ensure that whenever serious money is at stake, the two fighting birds will be equally matched. Over several games, everyone's wins and losses will even out—and no one will come away from a life of cockfighting much richer or poorer. A man's spirits might soar for a while, then, alongside his luck. But in the long run, his finances—and his future—are fixed; no amount of victory can alter his material status. As Geertz puts it in an essay published several decades later, titled "Deep Play: Notes on the Balinese Cockfight": "You cannot ascend the status ladder by winning cockfights . . . . Nor can you descend it that way. All you can do is enjoy and savor, or suffer and withstand, the concocted sensation of . . . movement . . . a kind of behind-the-mirror status jump which has the look of mobility without its actuality."

This is an excellent observation. In fact, it's the kind of observation that can propel a person out of academia's dusty sidelines and into the warm spotlight of general fame.

Following its publication, Geertz's essay is eagerly circulated across several continents. Soon, his name achieves a kind of sparkle when it is dropped into dinner party conversation, or stationed in long-form reviews amidst words of praise.

*Good for Geertz*, I think, when I hear this story. But what about the Balinese cockfighters? To my mind, they achieve a very different kind of renown: the intricacies of their lifestyle spread far and wide, prompting discussion in halls of learning. But no one ever hears them speak, since Geertz didn't interview them while constructing his theories. No one, in fact, even learns their names, because Geertz didn't deign to record them—leaving them to be erased by the passage of time, while his own transcends the slush pile of history.

So in one sense, the cockfighters do get to travel the world as abstract characters, changing the tenor of its debates. But I believe that only I can see the deeper, truer sense of the story—which is that functionally, anyway, they never get to leave their small village in the Global South. Or achieve the transcendence that is the birthright of other people.

I believe that they live and die, condemned to that old lot of the anthropological subject. The one so pithily expressed by Geertz himself:

"The look of mobility without its actuality."

# ROOM

Hui . . . what was that?

*A story, of course!*

But I wanted a story about you, to feel close to you again. This was about some random man named Geertz! And it was full of theories that made my head ache.

*Well, maybe I was going for something more interesting, you know? Higher order and intellectual, instead of frivolous like your run-of-the-mill story—*

But it wasn't fun to listen to!

*What exactly do you want, then?*

Why don't you describe what you did in Bali? Who did you even go with?

*Our parents.*

And our two younger brothers?

*No, they didn't join us.*

15

Well, tell me about the sights that you and our parents saw. Or about the people you met there, and how you felt about them.

*Ugh. How pedestrian.*

*But if you insist, I'll give it a go.*

# THE ISLAND PARADISE

## Continued

### III

DURING THE WEEK our parents and I spend in Bali, I think about Geertz and the unnamed cockfighters a lot.

Like on our first day there, when we check into our hotel. As the minivan pulls out of the leafy driveway, staff stream out to greet us in full *endek* dress: fabrics in deep greens and purples, rich patterns blossoming all the way down their torsos.

These people are barefoot and resplendent, resembling envoys from another century, when Bali was a mighty Hindu-Buddhist kingdom. On their faces hang the tender, benevolent smiles of nobility. "Would ma'ams and sirs like a drink?" one of them asks. Instantly, cups of ginger tea materialize on a carved wooden tray before us, along with the keys to our rooms.

In moments like this one, it's easy to believe that we have come to a land of courtly welcomes and lavish, gallant deeds. Not to an island wracked by socioeconomic inequality— where, just hours away from the glitzy south coast, villages in the north and east still lack clean drinking water.

The conceit is enticing. And yet.

And yet.

Over the next week, I watch as the hotel's staff dredge scum from swimming pools, tow suitcases, and cook omelets on demand for tourists' whining children. In the evenings, they squat by the hotel's back steps and smoke, fanning themselves with the faux-*udeng* caps that come with their uniforms.

One morning, I pass a member of staff crouched in the hotel lobby, sponge in hand. He's sopping up what looks like vomit from the hardwood floors; this part of Bali is blackout central, after all, where the wealthiest tourists get smashed every night. But as I look at the man's ankle-length, intricately patterned *endek* robes—now pooling majestically over the slimy floor—it dawns on me that the utility of his costume increases in proportion to the lowliness of his task. After all, a man scrubbing vomit from the floor in plain clothes may challenge the hard-earned impression that *this is an island paradise, where all can live in contentment and comfort.*

In a true paradise, one entertains liberally, asking nothing in return. Certainly one does not play host because one has to—or because one hails from a neighboring island with no electricity, with two young children to put through school.

A paradise becomes unworthy of the name if there should appear within it even one luckless creature. Perhaps this explains the local staff's clothes and smiles—their sustained efforts to play down the appearance of any discrepancy between themselves and their guests.

To create "the look of mobility" about themselves, without ever really achieving "its actuality."

· · ·

OVER A FEW days, Pak Andri, the minivan driver, becomes friendly with our father. This happens because they are both ethnically Chinese Indonesians—which is to say that their families survived several state-sanctioned genocide campaigns during the last seventy years.

At some point, it became too difficult to exist as Chinese people in Muslim-majority Sumatra—with the ever-present threats of discrimination, extortion, and, in extreme cases, race riots casting a pall over daily life. So each man's family gambled the present for its future. Our father's fled across several borders to Singapore, while Pak Andri's fled to Bali, another island in the country. Decades later, the two men occupy different stations in life: our father plays a minivan-hiring *tuan* to Pak Andri's salaried driver, or *supir*. But their shared memory of the gamble their families once took—and the national conditions of emergency that forced it—levels the playing field between them a little.

"This is too much," Pak Andri complains to our father. He announces this as our minivan rumbles past a large banner stirring in the breeze by the side of the road. The banner is bright red, bearing a slogan in block capitals: "TOLAK REKLAMASI TELUK BENOA" (Resist the Reclamation of Benoa Bay).

This is one of the first non-English signs we've seen all day, which makes me think that it's not for tourists. Or perhaps it's for a specific kind of tourist—the kind who's stayed here long enough to perceive that something isn't on offer to them, and who wants a part in it anyway.

Our father says: "Yes, the infrastructure in this place . . ."

And Pak Andri responds, one hand circling the steering wheel for eloquence: "Nothing ever stays good here. The roads, the land, the water . . ."

The road in front of us is marked by potholes; the banner speaks of problems that come from trying to reclaim land. What about water? I sprint through some figures: say there are five thousand hotels dotted around this island, plus hundreds of unregistered villas. And say that each one has a pool . . .

I think about all the news stories I read on international crisis-reportage websites before coming here. Impossible to describe how much of this island's water goes into making, and maintaining, the appearance of glamour. Each week, scores of foreign developers reach into Bali's south coast, summoning up yoga studios and restaurants by the dozen. Trump shakes hands with Hary Tanoe and a golfer's empire materializes, sun-bleached and thirsty by the liter.

But all this diverts water from the poorer north, where most locals live. In this land of glassy infinity pools, more than half the rivers have already run dry. Streams still crisscross the terraced rice fields of Ubud, where the tourists take their Instagram pictures. But deeper underground, the freshwater banks are pulling back from parched earth. Bali's farmers live the reality that its tourists cannot see—at night, they sleep in their fields with one eye open for irrigation thieves.

Later, I look around online for more stories about Benoa Bay. I learn that Tomy Winata, the Indonesian billionaire, is the one trying to reclaim land there. He wants to coax hectares of malls, theme parks, and a Formula 1 racetrack out of swampland. But this floating world will crush the coral reefs that protect Bali's coastline—reefs that keep the sea at bay. Eventually it will cause the island to flood, dragging whole villages into the sea.

In a tourist's kingdom like Bali, I reflect, the supply of pleasure must always meet the demand for it. Even if it costs the future for some people. Even if it means their deaths.

After all, this is paradise, where nothing is ever permitted to run out.

# ROOM

You're still not getting it.

*But I'm giving you what you asked for! Stories about places and people instead of academic theories.*

But now these sound like news stories! Reporting facts.

Why can't there be more adventure in your stories, Hui?

*Well—*

And feelings, too! You haven't said anything real about yourself yet.

*Give it a rest! You're so demanding, Nin.*

*I'll give you some drama, okay? And a part with anecdotes about me—my emotions, whatever.*

Go on then. I won't interrupt again.

# THE ISLAND PARADISE

## *Continued*

## IV

LET ME TELL you one last story about Bali. This time it's a creation story, concerning the very beginnings of paradise.

In this story, the year is 1906. Bali is an island divided. Dutch colonial forces have occupied the northern territories of the island, taking control of four of the eight kingdoms existing at the time. In this moment, they begin marching through the south to extend their dominion, winding from the shoreline of Sanur to the highest native court in the land, Klungkung.

This story is an old one whose basic tenets are familiar to many people around the world. At heart, it is a story about mismatched means and ends: guns versus *kris*, ambition versus ancestral claims.

The Dutch colonial troops pass quickly through the city of Kesiman to reach their first stop, Denpasar. A thriving market town and the capital of the kingdom of Badung, its streets seem far too quiet at first. Where is the resistance that the soldiers came ready to meet? But as they advance, they hear something stirring in the distance, from the direction of Denpasar palace: the faint but unmistakable pulse of drums.

The soldiers go on. As they near the palace, a procession of silent figures files out from its gates. From a distance, the soldiers spy the raja on his palanquin surrounded by courtiers and priests, wives and guards and children and servants. There are hundreds of people outside the palace now, robed in white with dusty feet. Tropical flowers laced into their hair.

Both parties, the Dutch and the Balinese, advance. Now there are two hundred paces between them; now, one hundred. The gap between two worlds is narrowing. Then it closes for the century to come, and possibly forever: a *puputan* commences.

The raja steps down from his palanquin and gives a signal. Instantly, someone from his own party lunges forward and knifes him in the chest. Motion erupts across the landscape as men force weapons into their own children, then stab themselves. Women fling jewels into the air and then topple, wailing, onto their knives.

Dark liquid fills the ground. A metallic scent rises. But Balinese people keep emerging from the palace in a slow, unstoppable stream. Once in sight of the Dutch troops, they plunge forward onto their daggers, then collapse into the growing snarl of limbs.

Their bodies cover the ground, both protest and decree.

By this point the Dutch soldiers have opened fire, then ceased fire, then opened fire again. They're panicking; they don't know what they ought to do. Several centuries of colonial rule have left them untrained for situations involving consent—and this seems like more than consent; this seems like some sort of perverse invitation. Eventually, they resort to doing what they know best—which is to seize what isn't on offer to them, looting the corpses for anything that gleams amidst the sticky mess of fluids.

There will be other *puputans* before Bali falls to colonialism completely, two years later. By then, the photographs of these mass suicides will have prompted moral backlash in Europe, with the thumping of Bibles and pontifical braying. Desperate to hold on to their empire amidst this PR disaster, the Dutch will announce a new resolution: from now on, they will protect Balinese culture and not gun it down. In fact, they resolve to protect Balinese culture so soundly that it never changes from its present state, or experiences the advancements of modern life.

*Let the world move slowly here,* their edicts declare. *Progress is not for the natives of this world—for the pure and innocent of heart.* Which is what the Balinese people are, presumably, violent *puputans* notwithstanding.

For decades to come, Dutch laws will force the Balinese people to wear *endek* dress and not linen pants—to converse in local dialects and not Malay, the regional code of anti-colonial rebellion. All over the island, atap roofs will sprout instead of modern innovations in galvanized iron. Whole dances will be invented for the Balinese people to perfect, then unleash upon large groups of visiting tourists—who, soon enough, will be everywhere, scouring the sights with their notepads and cameras, fresh from the war in Europe and hungry for brand-new visions of innocence to consume. *Look at this place,* they'll exclaim gleefully, pointing at random to rice fields and bare-chested women. *What authentic culture; what happy natives! So simple and content with their lot.*

They'll forget about the *puputans*, the cold carpet of bodies. The beginnings that made these visions possible.

In this manner, over the coming years, Bali's character will be formed. The eternal pleasure kingdom—of restaurants and hotels and F1 racetracks—will arrive, and stay.

Bali will become one of the most Instagrammable places on earth.

V

AS A HALF-INDONESIAN person, I grew up believing that I had an unusually complex relationship with places like Bali. In all the twenty-five years of my life, I had visited our father's country of origin only twice. Each time, however, I would feel myself entering a dream world whose colors and shapes were dimly familiar to me—breathy and warm in my mind, as if from some earlier moment of contact. To be part Indonesian, I imagined, was to be able to intuit the names of spices and fruits, unique varieties of rain. It was to recognize whole landscapes from the bedtime stories that our father used to tell us as children in Singapore—mountains and rivers, jungles lit up at night by tigers' eyes.

And so, when I come to Bali this time for a holiday with our parents, I start off with the assumption that I am not like the other tourists. After all, I have heard too many stories about this place and the country it is part of—I am already disillusioned; I have true clarity. I know all about this island's colonial wounds, the economic and ecological injustices of its present day. Unlike the other tourists, I am not to be duped; I am not here in search of some putative paradise. Because I understand that there are no so-called primitives here—only people like the ones who sit on my grandmother's porch back home in Singapore, reciting stock prices and exhaling *kretek* smoke late into the night. These are the Indonesian people whom I grew up among: no simple natives, but pragmatic citizens with the usual schemes and complex, calculating desires.

I assume that this knowledge will protect me while I travel through Bali; maybe even endear me to people. Instead I find myself needed, yet disliked—parsing the coolness that comes into people's eyes as I bargain with them in markets, or queue in the *kaki lima* outside their shops for breakfast. Always that familiar sense that someone wants to serve but not speak to me; that they are anxious for the cash register to ring so they can turn away from the counter and retract their smile.

*But I am not like the other tourists*, I want to protest, whenever this happens—whenever I try to speak in my halting Bahasa and am rebuffed in equally halting, dismissive English

*The anthropologists and partygoers might believe this is an island paradise where everyone lives in bliss. Where everyone is content to serve the outsider's gaze; to be turned into cultural, academic, or touristic spectacle.*

*But I am not like them—I am like you. I have the credentials of parentage on my side; I am an insider. I know all the stories.*

*I know how you really are. I know how you suffer.*

*I know that this is not a paradise at all.*

. . .

THE ENTIRETY OF our holiday passes in this vein. I win myself no friends; I make few happy memories. While our parents enthusiastically lounge on the beach, or stuff themselves full of food from various bars, I remain vocally incensed about everything I see: every row of nightclubs, every swimming pool. *No,* I protest, when they exhort me to join them; when they point out the fun that this place has to offer. *What's wrong with you? Don't you appreciate why this island is this way?*

*Can't you see that beneath the surface, it's awful?*

It isn't until many months later that something in me unravels. I'm not in Bali anymore by this time—instead I'm far away in Europe, where I've completed an expensive university degree. I'm tucked away in the grand modernist architecture of a high-ceilinged library, skimming a book called *A Small Place* by Jamaica Kincaid. All of a sudden I turn a page and there it is—the key—in the form of a passage that springs open before my eyes:

> That the native does not like the tourist is not hard to explain. . . . Every native everywhere lives a life of overwhelming and crushing banality . . . . Every native would like to find a way out . . . . But some natives— most natives in the world—cannot go anywhere. . . . [S]o when the natives see you, the tourist, they envy you, they envy your ability to leave your own banality and boredom, they envy your ability to turn their own banality and boredom into a source of pleasure for yourself.

The heat and rush of these sentences' inner truth. All at once it comes back to me: the gray Balinese skies, the humidity of October, and the humiliation of trying so hard to prove myself an insider on that little island—an island that I hadn't visited even once before. Hovering above are the outlines of a specific memory: Pak Andri's challenge to me on the day we first met, made so simply as to disavow—or at least disguise—its contempt.

*You want books for tourists?*

*Yes, Bahasa books. For tourists like you.*

I see, now, what he had been doing: putting me in my place. That, or offering me a generous gesture of guidance—some early indication of how I would be read there, regardless of the language that I tried to speak or the blood that ran, involuntarily, through my veins.

*You and I,* he was saying, *we are not alike.* I would never be able to be of the place, like he was.

I'm sinking down to the floor now, in between the library stacks in this faraway country. The book still wedged between my thighs as other scenes from the holiday resurface in my mind: the woman outside the bookshop, singing about New York City. I think about the arched contours of her voice—the vast and moving expanse of its emotions, which I had presumed to understand so well.

*Of course she feels bitter,* I had reasoned to myself, mentally reliving the stories I knew about Bali. Geertz and the cockfighters; the heat trail of dissent in the island's past. The farmers lying out in their fields at night, feeling the earth dry out beneath them, while only hours away, tourists smashed up some of Asia's top clubs.

In the singer's voice, I thought that I could hear what the anthropologists and other tourists wouldn't admit: that history had wronged this place, scoring its people with a deep sense of lack. But the truth is, I had no idea what I heard that day, lunging up from within the woman and brimming over the edge of her voice.

In all the ways that counted, I was as much an outsider to her as all the other tourists were. I wasn't equipped to tell if she was unhappy; I couldn't possibly know what she wanted. If she even wanted anything at all.

I shut the book in my lap. With my eyes closed, I see myself as I was on that sweltering afternoon in Seminyak Square: standing in the crowd with the other tourists, clutching my Lonely Planet guidebook. Listening to the music. Watching three musicians and a singer whose futures were fixed—tied to this island and its difficult fate.

All the while knowing, deep down inside, that I had the ability to leave this place. To turn it into paradise and then quit—like everyone else—when the pleasure finally ran dry.

Both the appearance of mobility and its actuality.

I was not like these people. I didn't know them at all.

# ROOM

*So? What did you think?*

My favorite part came at the end, when you finally talked about your feelings.

*I'm not sure I enjoyed doing that.*

But you have to do it, Hui.

That's the kind of story you need to tell in this room—about yourself, not theories or the news.

*Why?*

To help you remember.

*. . . What do you mean, remember—*

Anyway, my point is, I didn't like the first two parts of your story.

Listening to them felt like going to school.

*But that's what I was aiming for!*

To sound boring like a school?

*No—to be educational! To convey actual, important
information to other people, Nin. Not just regale them with
personal anecdotes.*

But I like those!

*They're frivolous. I'd rather my stories in this room have some
sort of . . . bigger vision to them. A political direction.*

Like a mission?

*Yes.*

I wonder what that could be.

*Well, what really got me going earlier was exposing the truth
about Bali. This faux-perfect place that everyone romanticizes—
when actually, it's downright riddled with problems.*

Looking pretty outside, but secretly damaged.

*Exactly. Carrying lots of burdens and baggage from its past.*

And you think it's important to keep talking about this
baggage?

*Of course! I guess you're still too young to understand this.*

*But in the world outside this room we're in—the real world of
grown-ups—it's critical not to idealize these problematic places!*

But why?

*Because when you wrap something broken in a beautiful
narrative, it becomes easy for others to overlook its mess instead
of addressing it. Meaning that systems can stay broken for a
really long time.*

Like years?

*Or decades. Maybe even forever.*

. . . Huh.

*You don't agree?*

. . .

*What is it—you think that I'm being overdramatic about this,
don't you?*

*But you're wrong! Because places like Bali—they ought to
upset you. They ought to make you want to scream until your
voice has ripped away that shiny façade and uncovered the raw
truth—*

Stop it, Hui! You're riling yourself up.

I only went quiet because I was thinking.

. . . *Oh.*

And I never said that I disagreed with you.

*Right.*

In fact, I was thinking that I can understand—why this topic feels so serious and important to you.

*To me?*

Yes—to you, specifically.

*Well, good.*

*But I think it should feel important to everyone, not only to me. Like in Bali—it made me so furious that our parents didn't care. Went on waltzing merrily around the beaches and restaurants, even though there were clearly all these problems under the surface.*

*You know, the two of them have always been like that!*

Like what?

*Clueless! Oblivious to reality.*

*Sometimes I feel like grabbing them by the shoulders and shaking them until they see.*

Maybe that should be the mission of your stories in this room, then.

*To shake up people like our parents?*

Yeah!

*Hm.*

*. . . I like that idea.*

*Telling stories about the reality of so-called perfect places. Or even about aspirational-looking people, or lifestyles—wrapped up in these too-shiny narratives. When really, they're problematic in all sorts of ways.*

I'd listen to those stories. As long as you keep filling them with lots of true details about your life.

That's all I care about.

*My personal anecdotes?*

Yeah.

*That's . . . kind of weird.*

*But hey, whatever floats your boat, I guess.*

Let's do it! I like the mission you've found for your stories.

*What should my next one be about?*

I don't know. But I think it should be one where you manage to discover the truth—not like with Bali, earlier.

*What do you mean?*

Well, at the end of that story, you said: "I was not like these people. I didn't know them at all."

That means you didn't get to find out the truth about them—right?

*I guess so.*

*When you put it that way, that story feels like such a failure. How midway through the telling, I realized that I had only a tenuous link to the place. And didn't actually qualify to speak about its culture . . .*

Because you'd never lived there?

*Yeah—and because our dad might be Indonesian, but we're not. I'm not.*

*I'm . . .*

Someone else.

*Yes.*

*I suppose I am.*

Your next story should be about something that you know personally.

*Like what, though?*

How about something that you have lots of experience
with?

*Hm . . .*

Or that you see every day? Or maybe even live with all the
time . . .

*I've got it!*

Oh?

*I know what story I can tell. One that fits the bill perfectly—
and also happens to be about a pretty juicy topic.*

I'm listening.

# HUI'S SECOND STORY

## *On Being in Love With a White Man*

### I

I FIRST MEET Thomas in the fall.

It is late in the morning, and the light is buttery. All across our campus, trees stagger under an excess of color; foliage falls to the ground in rich, soft bursts.

Thomas has just come out of the student hall's shared kitchen, holding a steaming mug of tea. He's wearing a rumpled college T-shirt. He has the blondest hair that I've seen on an adult man up to this point in my life—the blond of cherubs and country maidens, aglow in oil paintings.

"Do you want help?" he asks, watching me drag boxes down the corridor to my dorm room. It's my first day at this new university in Europe, eleven thousand kilometers away from my home in Singapore.

"No thanks," I tell him. "I can manage."

He nods, but stays put. Fifteen minutes later we're still chatting in the corridor, so I change my mind about the boxes. Thomas puts down his tea and comes over to help me lift them.

We add each other on Facebook. We date. And three years later, shortly before it's time for me to go back to Singapore for good, we decide to get married—so that I won't have to.


## II


THERE IS A template for how stories like mine should unfold. A white European man meets a Southeast Asian woman. In life, as in language, subject and object click neatly into place. Man and woman become the seeker and the sought-after; Europe and Asia, the explorer and the explored.

I grew up believing in the preordained nature of these roles. As a schoolchild in Singapore, I had learned that these pairings were rooted in history: our own nation had once been a mute but lovely island in Asia, waiting to be colonized by an Englishman named Stamford Raffles. Before his arrival, my teachers said, we had been nothing more than a primitive fishing village. Poor in some vital, existential sense that could not be ignored. But in other ways, we had been helpfully endowed with the right kinds of feminine traits—a beautiful form, for instance, and sunbaked slowness. A dripping, tropical fecundity.

For centuries, we seemed to do nothing but sit pretty on the equator, biding our time. Then one day, it all paid off. A European rounded the corner with a glint in his eye and delivered us to the world.

If pre-colonial Singapore taught me a sense of self, then Raffles furnished my earliest ideas about white men and what to expect from them. Sitting behind my desk and sweating into my school pinafore, I was captivated by the legacy of his desire. Here was the white man revealed as a glutton: gorging himself on the Other, sailing from shore to shore in hopes of consuming the world. I thought about the force of this desire, which had lifted us out of the darkness and into the bright lights of modern statehood. I thought about the little fishing village opening her mouth for the first time and finding out that she could speak.

*I am*, I imagined her saying, blinking into the light. *I am, I am.*

This story of Singapore's birth is over two decades old now. One rarely encounters it in circulation anymore—these days, the government's official line has shifted, so that the grade-schoolers are learning a very different tale of how their nation came to be. Their textbooks paint a picture that is seven hundred—not two hundred—years old; they read that the kingdoms of the world have been traipsing through our island since the fourteenth century, long before Raffles set sail.

Perhaps, then, they are also absorbing different ideas about desire: what it is and how it comes to be; who gets to wield it and who merely suffers it. I have my suspicions, though. A few years ago, at the state-funded bicentennial to celebrate Singapore's history, I seemed to recognize the previous story from my textbooks—lengthened by addendums, but otherwise unchanged. Earlier explorers were mentioned with more emphasis than usual, and other statues now rose to join the sculpture of Raffles that stands by the Singapore River. But ultimately, it was still Raffles who reigned supreme over the festivities—still Raffles who proved impossible to criticize. *How could we?* the glitzy public exhibitions seemed to ask, with a wringing of their hands. *How could we condemn the white man who imagined our city and pointed it in the direction of things to come?*

The struggle is to denounce that which, ultimately, ushered in our good and present selves. So we hold on to the white man who, in the midst of his greed, inadvertently showed us the way from Third World to First.

His landing is no longer a fiery dawning, or the ancient beginnings of the world. The white European man no longer declares the first fiat. Our new story is that he unleashes, or empowers, the land under his feet—releasing her into the life that she should have always had in the first place. His role has softened from that of a god into that of a catalyst—his presence figured as a necessary condition for the village to grow up and blossom in her own tanned skin.

In my own life, it is this second story that has proven truly insidious. Difficult to renounce, for standing so dangerously close to the truth.

### III

HERE IS THE portion of the truth that will surprise no one: I acquire new, formative experiences in the course of dating Thomas.

I learn to party, for example—to dance to minimalist techno, deadpan and delirious at the same time. I learn to make potato- and meat-based dishes whose names I can't pronounce, lavishly spiced with nutmeg and *kümmel*. And I learn to drink German schnapps one dusky evening, falling over myself in a tortuous mash of protest and laughter.

I cycle through Thomas's hometown in the Netherlands with him one day, the sun on our necks and the wind sluicing by. We're headed to a nearby lake, where I will wade in to my knees and squint at the sky, thinking: *True blue, like in a song or a poem. Genuine platonic blue.* "Clouds are just migratory lakes," Thomas will say. And it will strike me, in that moment, that I am having my first real experience of summertime—as distinct from the roiling, year-round heat back home. This is a new kind of sunlight that is blissful in its transience, registering the movements of the earth through time.

But there is another, less well-known, facet to the truth. Which is that the learning goes both ways, in the course of my relationship: Thomas also gains new experiences through me.

In general, Thomas and I garner very different kinds of comments when we speak about our sallies into each other's worlds. When I'm talking to other Singaporeans, my experiences tend to provoke the word "lucky" like a knee-jerk response—even when I'm describing the pallid, monotonous inner life of suburban-nowhere Europe. *So lucky*, my friends might say enviously, *I've never shopped at Aldi before!* As if Aldi could only be a huge step up from the NTUC FairPrices dotted around our island, location alone transfiguring the supermarket aisles into abundant and glowing repositories.

Through Thomas, people seem to imply, I have gained a free pass to a more rarefied domain. So of course, I am lucky; and of course, I should be grateful.

But no one ever applies these same words to my white European husband. Like me, Thomas has tripped his way across oceans and cultures to discover the banalities of a life elsewhere. But when other Singaporeans try to describe what he has done, the semantic field seems to wobble in confusion, and then settle around a completely different word than "lucky": "clever."

*So clever*, I've heard countless people say to Thomas over the years that we've known each other. *How come you know how to cook with this kind of chili! How come you understand Sin-glish! Who taught you to order kopi c bing—you sure you don't want Starbucks?* As they make these remarks, the look of wonder in their eyes always slides into the beginnings of a question:

*Why did you bother to learn this?*

The subtext here is altogether different. In adapting myself to Aldi and *kümmel*, I have only done what is expected of me, ascending the implied hierarchy. But in turning more Singaporean by degrees, Thomas has done something that worries people—and upon further reflection, might even come across as a form of subtle mockery to them. No Singaporean expects a white man to have studied our local quirks and habits, let alone to have committed them to memory for frequent, diligent application in daily life. After all, what does a person like Thomas gain from embodying the ways of our tiny nation, stuck on the tip of the Malay Peninsula? Our culture is a specialist pursuit, not some kind of global yardstick; our kopi is no Starbucks, and no one's measure of the good and civilized life.

The assumption, then, is that I must study Thomas's world as a debutante studies poise: eager to improve, and wary of slipups. Girlishly hoping to emerge transformed. Whereas Thomas is thought to observe my world as a specialist might observe a shiny new colony of ants: with interest, but with no intention of ever evolving in its likeness or direction. *Why would he want to?* whispers the sour voice in the back of our collective mind. *Why is this white man so desperate to become one of us; is he some kind of otaku loser?*

Maybe this is the issue with taking a relationship like mine and force-fitting it into the confines of a colonial found-ing myth. We assume that a white man, like Thomas, must always play the imperial pedagogue—a fully formed persona with established tastes and standards. Our story cannot hold space for the idea that he, too, might be an entity under construction—an ordinary man trying to peer beyond the horizon line of his own experiences in hopes of being changed.

Equally, our story can hold no place for a woman like me, who maps poorly onto the newborn and malleable island earth. What are we to do with a Southeast Asian woman who claims the role of the teacher, not the naïf—who wants to set the tone and infuse it with the tenor of her own beliefs? Who aims to be a progenitor of taste herself, and not merely a holding vessel for the tastes of other people—who wants to fashion the ground that she walks upon?

In this long, electric moment of contact between Thomas and me, who says that only one of us mandates the status quo? And who says that only one of us can suffer change— that only the island girl grows up?

. . .

HERE ARE SOME of the other activities that Thomas and I do while putting together the basics of a life:

We scroll through Singaporean meme pages on Instagram, cracking up at the shaky cellphone videos of middle-aged uncles misbehaving. We sit at the park near our house and people-watch in Singlish, so that we can make whip-smart comments that are mean but true.

We hoard used rubber bands and fold our plastic bags down into perfect origami triangles—channeling the gleeful frugality of two Nanyang-era grandmas. And we make lists of each other's favorite flavors from the bakery near my parents' house in Singapore, so that we can go hunting for close proxies in Chinatown in London, where we live.

We learn to communicate through staple Singaporean food items in lieu of saying "I love you." As we smother each other with sick-day congee and stalemate-breaking xiao long bao, it occurs to me that we are reaching that most dreaded milestone in the longue durée of coupledom: the point at which we turn into my parents.

On the morning that we get married, we arrive at the registry office a full hour before the doors even open, hoping to out-kiasu everyone else to the front of the queue. "Lame!" screams my friend from back home, laughing when I tell her about it later. "Y'all scared they run out of certificates or what?"

To people observing my relationship from the outside in, these moments may seem like nothing more than trivialities. But to me, at least, they are laden with potential—reminding me that decoloniality can reside in the details of everyday life, and not only in the bellowed edicts of governments and theorists. Power, after all, is that secret, glinting thread hidden within the fabric of experience: almost invisible to the naked eye, even as it holds together the many pieces of the world.

IV

THERE IS ONE more issue that I feel needs to be raised concerning this whole business of dating a white man as a Southeast Asian woman. Consider it a pressure point of sorts, pulsing and raw within the pathways of debate.

Shortly after Thomas and I got married, I came across an essay while doing my usual aimless rounds of late-night online browsing. This essay took the form of a letter, addressed by another Singaporean woman to her younger self. It contained advice that she wished this younger self had known at age eighteen, before she left home in Singapore for the hallowed grounds of Cambridge, in the UK, to attend university. And what it amounted to—in not so many words—was an instruction manual for decolonizing one's mind from the inside out.

In a fluid, beautifully limned series of anecdotes, the letter's author described how she had been humbled and impressed by her first brush with Cambridge. To her, its lofty bell towers had seemed to house the sublime; its Latin graces had seemed like sophistication versified. But she had not really understood, back then, where her own sense of awe had come from; it did not occur to her that colonialism lurked behind her belief that Cambridge's fish knives were a symbol of high culture, while the ixora flowers back home were not.

For years, the author wrote, she had naïvely parroted the belief that Singapore was inferior to Europe because it supposedly had less culture, less nature, less beauty. Only later did she realize that these terms were, in fact, loaded constructs, deviously formulated by the West to justify its own grip on power. And so she wanted to tell her younger self not to take these words too seriously—to squint past them in order to see the worth of her own culture and homeland. To understand that Europe didn't constitute the universe— so that a person like her could speak Singlish defiantly, and still deserve to be heard. She ought to be proud of what her country had made of her; to realize that she, too, could set the standards of achievement in this world.

All this was very rousing. But what really struck me had less to do with the letter itself, and more to do with a comment that had been left underneath it. In sentences that sparked and shimmered with barely controlled fury, somebody had written the following indictment of the woman behind the piece:

> The irony of it all is that [she] has married a white dude . . . and is now a citizen of the United States.
>
> She will have half-white kids, who will deny they have ANY Asian blood and [will] speak perfect American English. [The author] laments [the loss of] a culture she is only too eager to shed.

I detected, of course, the familiar whiff of colonial logic in these accusations. What made this stranger so sure that the author would naturally assimilate away from her own background—raising her kids in perfect American English, instead of in the register of las and lors? Knowing this didn't stop the sudden, scalding thought that came as my cursor hovered over the comment: *Is this person right? Can I ever talk about decoloniality—and act like I'm on the right side of history—if I'm married to a white man? If I've chosen to live with him in Europe?*

There ought to be a name for concerns like this one, which reside somewhere in the perilous borderland between theory and praxis. Since meeting Thomas, I have spent more time than expected grappling with them—smelting them down over and over again in a futile attempt to derive even the tiniest trace of personal conviction.

Because the thing is: I know all of the theoretical arguments that exist to deconstruct and diagnose the situation I am in. I've thumbed through my Edward Said and Homi K. Bhabha like any good scholar from the equator; read a million different riffs on Edwin Thumboo's poems. So I really do know the credos that can be summoned in the postcolonial tropics in aid of poesis. I know that our banyan trees are solemn and regal as they hold up the sky, and that the sunset over this part of the world speaks a language of its own. That most of the dreamers on the continent will wash up on Singapore's shores eventually, muttering their incantations of hope and power in a hundred mother tongues. I have been that teenager trying to spin poetry out of national policy changes, and photographing the stern, brutalist edifices that tower briefly over Singapore like gods, before vanishing into the open jaws of capital. I know that there is great beauty at work there, on my island—that the place I come from is a wide and generous breadbasket of the imagination.

And yet there is a gulf between this knowledge and the place where desire lives in me—between what I know I should want, and what I actually do want. Call it the gap between "desire" and desire—one a black-and-white term in a textbook, and the other that messy feeling that arises in me at the sight of my husband in his ratty college hoodie, checking his emails on the couch. Call it the reason why so many decolonial theorists—in spite of the counsel of their better selves—still live and work in the West today; why Singaporean women like the letter's author and me might write fiery little essays, but then swipe right on the usual suspects, or come home to the white men we have married.

When it comes to the issue of dating white men, we'd like to think that desire must always imply some deficiency in the status quo. We assume that a Singaporean woman does it because she has swallowed the colonial myths and no longer appreciates the country that she comes from. To this, I say that desire—when it comes from the hot gut and not a place of calculation—proves nothing at all, beyond the existence of itself. I do not want to be with Thomas because he is better than some politically correct alternative that could exist. I want to be with him because he is who he is. And I cannot help wanting to be with him, despite knowing what I do about the picture that we make—even though I know that our bodies, walking down the street, will instantly cease to be our own; that they will turn into vessels for the usual play of power.

It is true, of course, that our yearnings can often be traced back to gnarled and blighted places within us—places whose very existence we might regret. But for all that we know about the impurity of desire's origins, the heart of the matter is that it will always remain wretchedly, utterly ungovernable. Even in a place like Singapore, it is incapable of bending to political dictums about what should and shouldn't be allowed. We desire the wrong bodies all the time for the politics that we hope to have; we retweet the right beliefs, and then imagine the wrong faces in the darkness of our bedrooms. The sarong party girls will go on—forever and always—kissing the wrong sorts of men, kicking themselves in the heart, then going out the next day to do it all over again.

Because the point is, really, that they don't do anything in life for the sake of responding to that all-pervasive narrative— the one about the explorer and the island. Women like us don't exist solely to validate Singapore's myths about itself— or, for that matter, to refute them. Our shoulders are too busy dancing to hold the weight of that hoary nationalist burden; we're too busy chasing our ambitions to stand still in a line-up and function as our country's exemplars. We want too much from life, you might say, to play the part—to be the good women vigilantes, safeguarding national culture through the medium of our bodies.

The fact is that we want the way that men have, generally, been allowed to want: endlessly and effortlessly, heedless of ourselves. Madly, extravagantly beyond the pale. And if this means that we eventually marry the white men who buy us drinks or move us into our dorm rooms, then so be it. Let desire be; let it stand testament to nothing but itself. No other hearts are burning here but ours.

# ROOM

*That was much better, wasn't it?*

Yeah! You shared so much more about your life in that story.

*. . . Sure. But that's not what I mean.*

*I'm talking about my mission in this room—remember?*
*Showing the truth behind aspirational places and people?*

Oh . . . that.

*This time, I really got to sharpen my claws! And dig them hard*
*into the outdated colonial fantasies—*

Ah.
*—tear right through them, to reveal the stark truth about living*
*in a marginalized, racialized, fetishized body—*

You did very well, Hui. Much better than with your first story.

*Thank you!*

Just wondering, though—what sort of white person is
Thomas, actually?

*. . . What?*

He seemed a bit mysterious, that's all. You said something about drinking German schnapps with him—but then about his hometown being in the Netherlands. And you also mentioned Chinatown in London?

> *Right. I could have been clearer about that: nationality-wise, Thomas is German. But he grew up in the Netherlands, and we met and live in England now.*

And what else is he like, besides being a white man?

> *Excuse me?*

Well, you mentioned that one fact about him so many times. But I was curious about other aspects of him too, like . . . mm . . . what's his favorite color?

> *Uh . . .*

And what kinds of animals does he like? What kinds of TV shows?

> *Why on earth do you need to know this stuff?*

I'm curious! And maybe you've forgotten, but I'll never get to meet Thomas.

> *That's true.*

So tell me more—what are his hobbies? And does he have any big dreams he wants to achieve?

*I . . .*

*I'm not sure why, but I'm feeling very anxious about this swarm of questions.*

No need to answer, then! How about an easy one: Overall, what do you like most about Thomas's personality?

*. . . I don't know.*

Really?

*It's hard to say, okay? He's just a nice guy.*

Meaning?

*His personality is kind of . . . like . . . agreeable, you know? Normal? Fine? Pleasant enough?*

*And anyway, the most important thing about Thomas is that he helped me to get a British spousal visa! So I didn't need to ship back home to Singapore again. But this was all in the story— why are you making me dredge it up?*

I thought—

*You know, Nin, I really don't like it when you interrogate me like this! About the details of my life outside this room—my marriage, my husband, his personality traits . . . Honestly, it's ridiculous. Such a massive waste of time.*

Why, though?

*Because it almost feels like you're giving me a test!*

*And sure, I might be failing the test—really obviously and badly. But so what? For fuck's sake—who even cares what Thomas is like, outside of his race? That's the only part of him that matters for my stories!*

*Why can't we focus on that?*

Okay, okay! Don't stress out.

I won't ask about Thomas again.

*Good!*

*You'd better not.*

But Hui—

*What now??*

Nothing! Not a question.

I only wanted to say I feel glad you married Thomas.

*. . . Why?*

Because you two sound very happy together.

*Really?*

Yes. Even though it also sounds like you can't see him very well.

*. . . Huh.*

*"Happy" is such a relative term.*

What do you mean?

*It's just that . . .*

What?

*Oh fuck it, Nin. All your stupid questions.*

*They've made me recall what got left out of the story—that outside this room, Thomas and I aren't happy at all.*

You're not?

*No. Our relationship has been bad for a while.*

But what about all the wonderful moments you described? Where you read memes, or people-watch?

*Sometimes we still have those. But nowadays, we also spend a lot of our time together . . . fighting.*

Really?

*Yes. Screaming, and slamming doors, shoving our fingers in each other's faces—*

Gosh! You didn't mention that.

*Of course not—because it's mortifying! And it's not like that side of our relationship really fit in the story.*

So . . .

How often do you and Thomas . . . you know.

*Fight? Every day.*

*Sometimes more than a few times a day, actually. If you really want to know.*

That sounds so rough. What do you fight about?

*My god. I don't know.*

*On one level, it feels like we're always fighting about the political issues in the story: race, society's expectations, colonial baggage, blah blah. How I moved fucking continents for the sake of our marriage. How I have to fend off so much judgment.*

*But you know, sometimes when our fights get really, really bad, I . . .*

You what?

*. . . I wonder if I even know anymore. What we're fighting about.*

That's weird.

*It's just that I get these flashes of doubt sometimes. Midway through our fights, when we're screaming all the usual words—and then suddenly I'll get this feeling like . . . it's all not real, or something.*

Not real?

*Yeah. Like I'm in character.*

Playing a part.

*Exactly—like I'm only going through the motions. And it's strange, because of course I mean the words I'm saying—about racial injustice and all the ways I'm suffering as an Asian woman.*

*But it also feels like there's something else beneath the words—something sort of . . . older.*

You mean like the fight is familiar to you?

*Yes! Almost as if I've done it all before.*

*And that's when I get scared and make mistakes.*

Like what?

*Well, one time recently, I . . .*

You?

*. . . Never mind.*

What did you do, Hui?

*I just—I don't feel like saying it out loud.*

But you know it'll never get beyond this room. It's not like I can repeat it to anyone.

*. . . Fine.*

*I threatened Thomas with a kitchen knife, okay? We were fighting over something dumb again—some toothache I had. That he didn't notice, that he didn't help me to make a dentist appointment for.*

*The fight started small, and then it got bigger. Became a torrential shouting match about me moving to Europe and him not deigning to help me navigate the system here . . . at some point, I reached out and grabbed the biggest knife that I could see on the kitchen counter. Aimed it at Thomas and screamed until he left the flat.*

*When he came back, a few hours later, he cried on our couch in his college hoodie. The one that I mentioned briefly, in the story.*

Wow.

A lot gets left out of your stories, huh?

*Am I a bad person, Nin?*

. . .

*You think I am, don't you? That's why you're not replying.*

. . .

*And maybe you're right, you know? Maybe I am a bad person, and also a bad wife. I honestly don't know why I did that to Thomas with the knife. Sometimes I feel so ashamed of the way I treat him that I wish I could die—*

Hui, don't spiral. It's okay.

I don't think you're a bad person.

*. . . Really?*

Yes. But I do have a question: Why are you always here in this room with me?

*What do you mean?*

I mean—why are you here now, instead of outside in the real world? Talking to Thomas?

*I don't . . .*

*I don't know.*

*Sometimes I wonder if that's part of the problem with my marriage.*

That you're always in this room?

*Yes—under this ceiling fan. Lying on this one small mattress that we share. And brewing up stories instead of facing the outside world.*

You know that you can leave this place, right?

*Yeah. But I don't want to.*

*For now, at least, I have this feeling—like I need to be here. Even if it's dangerous. Or destroys what's left of my marriage.*

Why?

*I can't explain it. I just feel like if I leave too soon, something that's here with us will be lost.*

*Something that I'm . . . looking for.*

. . . Hui?

*Hm?*

You look sad. Will you tell me another story?

*Okay. What should it be about?*

How about another topic like the previous ones? To look at what's underneath perfect people, or places.

*Is it all right if the story is sad?*

Tell me.

I can take it.

# HUI'S THIRD STORY

## *The Sad Girl Variations*

## I

THE MIND IS nothing but dust, groping its way towards iridescence.

On good days, it can feel like my own has found its sheen at last. The thoughts pile up, pulsing and bright and quick. Feelings arrive without effort; colors and sounds seem to burst behind my skull.

But then there are the other days—the ones where my mind goes back to being dust. Like today, for example: gray on gray on gray. Thomas leaves the house at nine in the morning while I'm still asleep. When he returns after the sun has set, I am still in bed. Lying as I was left—unwashed, unfed, and undone.

He lies down next to me, eyes to the ceiling. Voice very still, as is usual for these occasions: "Not one of the good days, huh?"

The dust circles down from my head into my mouth and crowds out the beginnings of an answer.

LIKE MANY OTHER women of my generation, I grew up in the blogosphere, under the aegis of the Melancholy Tumblr Girl. If our demographics overlap in any way whatsoever, then you probably recognize the character I mean: long pale limbs, prominent cheekbones. Big mournful eyes that look permanently brimmed over, their expression forever poised on the brink of some precipice.

The Melancholy Tumblr Girl had many ink-on-paper forerunners, like Ophelia by the lake or penitent Mary Magdalene. The women splayed across most editions of Lang Leav's books, cupping their ivory cheeks in their hands. Online, though, she tended to conform strictly to a type. For instance, she was nearly always white—although she could also be East or Southeast Asian, like me. The important thing was for her to skew fair, and thus fragile—like a beautiful, bruisable canvas of a woman, translucent in the spotlight. Her skirts were always floaty, like wraparound gauze. And her face was always half-hidden from view—turned to the ground amidst shadows, or buried behind a handful of wildflowers. The effect being to tantalize the gaze; to articulate something like *Noli me tangere, but hey, also, rescue me.*

In the hundreds of thousands of photos of her that existed online, the Melancholy Tumblr Girl was always posed against lush dreamscapes too perfect to exist in actual time and space. Like a cornfield saturated in deep blues and yellows, or a petal-strewn clearing in the woods. Beyond these photographs lay snippets of pathos-laden text by other famous Sad Girls across the ages: Anne Sexton and Sylvia Plath, Emily Dickinson. From Dickinson: "And I am out with lanterns, looking for myself."

The Melancholy Tumblr Girl taught me that sadness was a pose you could wear to great effect, if you happened to inhabit a certain kind of female body. If you happened to have a certain kind of fawn-legged grace. I became obsessed, scouring the edges of Tumblr for pictures of her to drag and drop onto my own blog. At school, I scoped out the girls who fit the type and observed them from afar. Noticing their delicacy and their pale, perfect skin; the way that admirers clustered around them like insects around the wet, open center of a flower. I saw how their sadness seemed to waft around them like a scent, never once manifesting in that ugly, raw-meat color that my own face would turn after my increasingly frequent bouts of crying, balled in the corner of my bedroom alone, tears coming down my face for no apparent reason.

What I felt in those moments was a ragged physical urge, not the cause-and-effect logic of ordinary sadness. A tightening of the chest; the sour edge of a key twisting slowly in my gut. All the same, I knew that I would never quite qualify as a Melancholy Tumblr Girl. I was too chubby and too short, too prone to unglamorous physical realities like sweat. Too easily enthused; too easily intrigued by the minutiae of the world around me.

I couldn't do lithe; couldn't do spectral. My crying, I knew, was going to have to find another name for itself in order to qualify as a woman's route to power.

### III

BY MY LATE teens, I'd moved on from the assorted Sad Girls of the internet. Now, instead of Melancholy Tumblr

Girls, I fixated on Melancholy Girls from the history of the church—in particular, the French mystic and philosopher Simone Weil. Having turned more seriously religious around this time, I was making my way through the usual range of books for the thinking and questing faithful: C. S. Lewis, G. K. Chesterton, Henri Nouwen—whose Catholicism was treated as a strange, but tolerable, aberration by my own staunchly Protestant church in Singapore. *I guess that it's okay to read him*, a pastor once told me, *as long as his books can uplift your spirit. God can speak through anyone, you know?*

By these standards, Simone Weil fell patently short of my church's recommended reading list. She may have been one of Europe's best-known philosophers, and one of the canon's only women to boot. But her essays were bereft of any intention to uplift the spirit—to clarify, buoy, or otherwise make more bearable the experience of faith. Also, I was not quite sure that the voice in them belonged to God. The pages threw out his name incessantly, of course. But somehow the force animating them still seemed to be Weil's own—issuing forth from her wild and bumbling, myopic person to shoot down through the decades like a clear stream of fire.

I fell in love with the voice in these books, and read them on the sly without consulting my church. Scrolling through the PDF of *Gravity and Grace* when I couldn't sleep at night: "Two forces rule the universe: light and gravity." The cadence of this sentence was enough to make me cry.

But then, in those days, nearly everything was enough to make me cry. I cried in public worship sessions a few times a week—once on Sunday mornings, and once at the beginning and end of each youth meeting on Saturday. I cried in the prayer groups that the pastors corralled us into—mouth moving fast, heat seeping out of my eyes as I tried to control my breathing. And I cried for at least an hour most evenings after school, rocking with my legs crossed behind a locked door. Doing what my church referred to, charmingly, as "quiet time"—my parents' guitar perched on my lap, a Bible flipped open at random in front of me. My mouth giving shape to a knowable, ownable narrative about my tears, and slinging it along the contours of melody:

*In my weakness / your power can shine*
*In my weakness / I see your grace and your might*

*Drawing close to God,* I would have said, if anyone had asked me what these sessions were about. Running my fingers along the wet and swollen seams of my eyes: *I guess that the spirit really moved in me today.*

Weil, too, was convinced that the spirit really moved in her. Like so many Sad Girls before her and since, she believed that her despair was full of purpose—a true and gilded path to glory. "[E]very time that I think of the crucifixion of Christ," she wrote in a letter to the priest J. M. Perrin, "I commit the sin of envy." Her whole life was an attempt to bear out this competition by finding newer and better postures of distress to embody—sacrificing herself for the sake of the collective. In childhood, she began by refusing small pleasures in solidarity with France's suffering troops in World War I: turning down sugar, sending away socks. Then came her adult attempts to douse herself in misery—often to the point of comedic excess, so that her wealthy family had to swoop in to rescue her. She took up hard labor on factory lines and bumbled her way into Spain's civil war. As a Jew in the throes of World War II, she tried—and failed—to get sent behind the front lines in what essentially amounted to suicide missions.

But her most famous act of suffering, by far, was her lifelong refusal to eat enough food. She pushed away perfectly good meals in disgust and, when necessary, chewed like a person suffering from toothache. Wincing as though each bite were a struggle—shameful in its revelation of mammalian need. In her essays, she embroidered whole theologies around this particular revulsion: framing starvation as an act of so-called "decreation," which hollowed out her soul to receive God's grace. Or as a gesture of divine solidarity, professing her support for France's malnourished troops. To be emptied, said Weil, was to be made pure; in fact, science ought to find a way to nourish people on sunlight, so that they never needed to eat again.

When she died at age thirty-four in a sanatorium, her most pertinent cause of death was listed as cardiac failure from self-starvation—even though she'd also been suffering from a severe case of tuberculosis. Her frame was so light that the coroner's report boiled down to an accusation: "The deceased did kill and slay herself by refusing to eat." In other words, this was a woman in thrall to some pathology of the mind that had finally laid waste to her gaunt and ailing flesh.

But here is the thing about being a Sad Girl of the faith, like Weil was, and like I used to be. Religion has so many alternative words for sickness—and Christianity, in particular, is adept at renaming it. The early saints had fits and called them high visions; the medieval virgins scored their flesh and called it emulation. And so, like countless other Sad Girl saints across time, Weil became an icon precisely because she suffered. *Her starvation was her genius*, said her legion of admirers—proof that she accepted Schopenhauer's concept of the will. Proof that she had, after all, really known divinity—felt it rush through her like the wind through a sail.

Her starvation became a symbol first, and a bodily experience second—she starved herself, they said, for the wretched of the earth. In solidarity with the hungry and hurting across Europe. And so "she died of love," her first English biographer wrote, capping off the scene with a grand and gothic flourish. As if there were no chemistry to account for at all; as if there were nothing dangerous twisted into the mix.

Is it still a disorder if you're doing it for God? If you're spouting tears; if you're starving yourself? Today, people on the internet remain unsure, much like they were when I was a teenager. *Simone Weil wasn't sick*, the hardliners tend to shout, from the safety of their footnoted paragraphs. *Extreme* they can concede; even *touched by madness*. But to mention OCD or anorexia is pushing it too far for them, lumping the lambent in with the dust. These mental health conditions seem almost schoolgirlish to them, like diagnoses that should be framed by the qualifier "mere." Unbefitting of a thinker so brilliant and profound; so influential in shaping the world that came after her.

But the Sad Girls like me, we know better. We smell our sister under the skin. We know that if you're a certain kind of woman, like Weil, then the deal that the world gives you isn't power or sickness. As if you could only hold on to one or the other. Instead, power and sickness so often come together for us—wrapped up in age-old beliefs about female flesh. About its weakness and capacity to be more easily influenced; its relative permeability to both evil and the divine. Think of Eve in the garden, her chin wet with juices; Mary sitting rapt at the feet of God. The mothers in our churches who minister as intercessors—open to power, porous to the light. Trembling as the word of God punctures them like a sword.

We understand how faith can turn us into conduits, vessels for something outside of ourselves. And in doing so, rename our susceptibilities—the ones that we might struggle to find our own words for. Like our proneness to tears, say, or to visions or frenzy. Faith can dress these tendencies up to resemble devotion—turn them useful and even productive. Like attributes that we could, conceivably, harness towards self-fashioning—so that we feel chosen instead of merely damaged. Radiant to the degree that we raise our hands and suffer.

So that we make peace with the fact of our suffering. Instead of asking if we should be suffering at all.

"Grace fills empty spaces," Weil wrote in *Gravity and Grace*, the book of hers that I loved best. "[B]ut it can only enter where there is a void to receive it, and it is grace itself which makes this void."

I turn back to read this sentence again, a decade after I first encountered it. And I think about how the word "void" could be swapped out for a second-degree synonym that has echoed through my own life as an adult:

*But grace can only enter where there is depression to receive it.*

*And in some ways, it is grace itself which makes and maintains this depression.*

## IV

AFTER I LEFT the church in my early twenties, I didn't know what to do with my tears anymore. Christianity had structured my catharsis for so long, giving me permission to snivel and cry. Over my guitar, over lifted palms; once every day, and even more on the weekends. But now, without this framework to fall back on, the tears assailed me all the time. They sprang to my eyes in alarmingly public places, like at my office desk or in supermarket aisles. As I waited to cross at busy intersections, so that people across the street would gawk.

I tried to ignore the tears for as long as I could. But then something began to shift inside me: my compulsion to cry began, inexplicably, to morph. Over time, it hardened into something that felt much closer to fatigue than sadness—a numbness so deep that it seemed almost cellular. The feeling would arrive early in the morning, as my thoughts absorbed the first pale flickers of consciousness. And then it would spool out as the day dragged on—endlessly gray, endlessly flat. Endlessly long and wide and empty.

By this stage, I would have missed the textures of sadness had I felt capable of missing anything at all. Instead, I lay in bed whenever it was possible and stared at the ceiling above me for hours. Sometimes my eyes still leaked a little moisture, as if my body were begrudging a reflex. But overall, the weight in my bones flattened out most of my extant desire to cry. Emotions felt far too tiring to attempt, with their visible postures of excess and deficiency. Their clumsy, fleshly efforts at communication.

I was becoming, in other words, the opposite of a Sad Girl: I was becoming a woman who couldn't perform her emotions at all.

Here is the realization that I keep coming back to, when I think about the Sad Girl's influence over the past decade of my life. The Sad Girl may have seemed to sit close to depression, with her lowered eyes and smoky melancholia. Her varied, alluring poses of affliction. But the truth is that in every way that counted, she behaved differently than an actual depressed person would. Unlike them, she was obsessed with curating her image—arching towards her audience in earnest and straining to see herself through its eyes. *Am I interesting?* she was constantly asking, with misery poised over her features just so.

*Does my suffering mean something to you?*

Depression may have looked a lot like the Sad Girl, but it left me incapable of asking such questions. On bad days, it drained my desire to project a self at all—to care about being seen by, or meaning something to, anyone. I felt no compulsion to speak or get dressed; to perform all the small actions that could cohere my person. *What for?* asked the illness, uncoiling behind my eyes. *What is the point of attempting your own existence?*

Perhaps another way to put it is this: the Sad Girl, unlike me, was ardent and alive. She moped a lot in the pictures, sure. She starved and hurt and writhed and swooned. But all this suffering was, ultimately, on account of her passionately wanting things—like attention or even devotion. The warmth of our gaze; feminine cool. This made her different from the truly depressed person, whose mind is incapable of summoning up desire. For me, depression felt like the very antithesis of wanting, as if all the aspiration had been leached from my being. Like some vital part of me had been swaddled, so that no more zeal could graze its surface. Nothing could interest me when I was in this state—not one item in the Sad Girl's long list. I would have shrugged off her whole litany of yearnings. Assured her, blandly, that none of it mattered.

My point is that the Sad Girl did have a relationship with mental illness—only not the one that we often assume. She wasn't responsible for turning girls depressed, as if her glamour somehow convinced us to suffer. Instead, the Sad Girl's real fault was in being so misleading—in touting a mental state that seemed similar to depression, but was actually its inverse. Her crying face was, functionally, a kind of decoy. And being such a culturally valued decoy, it occupied all the discursive space that depression should have held for us. Caused us to grow watchful for all the wrong signs: for tears and not tiredness; excess, not nonchalance. For beguiling visions in long peasant skirts, floating about in silky despondence. Using their suffering to make a point. Not people in sweat-stained pajamas, pinned to their beds by an invisible weight. Struggling to eat their one meal of the day; struggling to care about making any point at all.

The Sad Girl was, essentially, a beautiful distraction, one that occupied too much space in our collective mind. Causing us to neglect our real enemy, as it stood there waiting for us with hunger in its eyes.

Nowadays, you might think, we finally know better. So much mental health information is eddying all around us—in the magazines we read and the media we swipe through. In the state-sponsored ads on our bus stops and trains, reminding us to please take care of each other. But how much have we really learned, I wonder. How far have we come from what the Sad Girl represented? It's true that misery no longer seems to have the same aesthetic hold on us—the Melancholy Tumblr Girl is on her way out now, sinking into the cold depths of internet history. But consider the new feminine ideal that is taking her place: the glowing, pony-tailed woman of wellness, holding yoga poses in her breathable tights. Wholesomely, admirably strong and trim; diligently Thermomixing her way to health.

Why does this wellness woman always look so happy? In every single ad, she beams like the sun itself is juicing through her pores; as if she's the emissary of some special golden bliss. She looks so uniformly, persistently euphoric that I can't help but wonder: Is she to today's teenagers what the Sad Girl once was to me? A red herring towering over us all, holding out half-truths about mental health? If the Sad Girl misinformed me that depression looked like sadness, then perhaps this new icon does something similar, by telling today's girls that wellness looks like happiness. As if psychiatric health could only ever express itself one way, in the guise of a smiling face.

If depression is nothing like sadness, it stands to reason that its opposite isn't happiness. Rather, the opposite of being depressed is being able to really, really feel—emotions like hope and joy and comfort, yes. But also ones that might be, traditionally, classed as negative: woe and fear, loss and pain. Luminous rage. Tidal grief.

Each one of these feelings is proof that you're alive. Proof that the world can still get under your skin and arouse the necessary commotions inside you. So each one of these feelings is a strike against depression; each one, in its own way, is a step back from the edge. A tentative step in the direction of true wellness; progress forward on a long and winding road.

Even the sadness. Even the tears.

The saddest girl of all is the one who never cries.

# ROOM

Sorry to hear you get sad like that, Hui.

*It is what it is.*

Why don't you ever cry in this room, though?

*. . . I don't like doing it in front of other people.*

Even me?

*Yes. That's what I needed church for when I was growing up. To help me cry in a way that no one would notice.*

But what's wrong with them noticing?

*I don't feel good about it! Even now, if I imagine someone watching me cry, I don't feel like they're going to be kind.*

What do you feel?

*I feel . . . afraid. Kind of chilly in my bones, like something painful might be about to happen.*

That's terrible. If I cried, I'd want someone to realize right away and rescue me.

. . . How come Mum and Dad never did that for you?

*Rescued me?*

Yeah. Because you cried at home, right, when you lived with them?

*Well—I was in our bedroom, where they couldn't see me.*

But you said that you did it every day! And for a whole hour. Wouldn't they have noticed if your eyes were always swollen?

*I mean—*

Or if your face was always turning blotchy and red?

*Whoa, whoa—*

And come to think of it, with the layout of our house, wouldn't the sound have traveled straight through our walls, into Mum and Dad's room?

*Hold on, Nin!*

*Are you saying that I exaggerated the crying?*

. . .

*I feel like that's what you're insinuating—that those years couldn't have been that bad. Or that I had only an ordinary dose of sulky teenage hormones. But I didn't, okay, and I don't know what I have to say to make you take me seriously—*

No, Hui. I believe you.

I believe that you really suffered in those years.

*Then what are you saying?*

Just that . . . it's interesting how Mum and Dad didn't respond to you crying. Almost as if they were already used to it.

*. . . What?*

*What do you mean?*

That maybe by the time you were a teenager, our parents were already expecting you to cry like that at home. Daily.

*That's ridiculous!*

Is it?

*Of course! I'm sure they thought what I did—that I was getting emotional because of my daily quiet time.*

*And anyway, what would I even have been crying about, before I became a teenager?*

Being a kid, I guess.

*But I had such a boring childhood. In fact, it was so boring that I've forgotten large chunks of it—*

Oh!

Is that why all your stories so far have been focused on your adult life?

*Yeah. I've lost most of my memories from the years before that.*

*. . . What? Hey, why are you looking at me that way?*

It's just . . .

I don't think that's normal. To have forgotten so much of your own life.

*Nah—lots of people have these sorts of big unexplained memory gaps. And mine aren't even that bad. I can remember a lot from my very early years—up to when I was the same age that you are, here. Seven or eight?*

And then you have a hole?

*Well, it's more like the picture that was so detailed before . . . fades away. Becomes this gray, trembling surface for a while . . . until suddenly it snaps back into focus, only a decade has passed and I'm now sixteen. The crying, blogging teenager from the story.*

Wait—do you mean your Tumblr era? That didn't happen till you were sixteen?

> *Yeah. For a year or so, before I got obsessed with Christian books instead.*

That wasn't clear from your story at all!

> *No?*

No. You said you "grew up" blogging. So it sounded like you had the blog when you were nine or ten, and had lots of other memories from that age . . .

Why were you so vague about your age, Hui?

> *I don't know.*

Were you trying to hide your memory gap?

. . . Maybe you're not that comfortable with it. Even though you say you are.

> *Look, Nin. I don't think that anything is wrong because I'm missing a few little memories, okay?*

You don't think it's messed up?

> *No! That's just how it works for me!*

Okay, okay. No need to get angry.

Tell me more about your life after sixteen.

*What's there to say? I was a giant nerd.*

*Besides going to church, all I did was study in our bedroom. Plod through practice papers and compute equations, rote learn essays to regurgitate in exams . . .*

And you enjoyed that?

*Of course not! I only wanted to get good grades.*

Why?

*I knew that if I did well in my international exams, our parents might send me to a university abroad. Lots of other Singaporean parents were doing it at the time—and it looked like my only ticket out of that soul-destroying country.*

But I thought you liked it there! Weren't you proud of being Singaporean?

*Culturally—and in theory, for the sake of my stories—sure. But in practice, I hated growing up there.*

Why?

*Well, for starters—*

Wait, was it because of the same thing that made you get depressed?

*. . . What?*

Well, something made you cry every day, right? When you were living in Singapore?

*Jesus, Nin.*

*Why are you spouting nonsense again?*

*I thought I made it clear in the story—nothing "bad" ever happened. Depression is simply an illness that appears for no reason. To people who get unlucky with their brain chemistry.*

So you wanting to leave Singapore—it had nothing to do with the crying.

*No! It was all about intellectual principles for me! Because I couldn't stand the politics of that place: the authoritarianism, the hypercapitalism, and the criminalization of queer bodies at the time—not like you even understand what all those words mean—*

Mm.

*—and of course, there was the education system!*

You sound like you hate that one the most.

*Damn right! Singapore—it had one of the world's harshest education systems when I was growing up! Insanely stressful. With endless exams, and cram schools on the weekends—on top of schooldays that already ran from sunrise to 10:00 PM—*

That sounds so extreme.

*It was! Kids there were way more anxious and depressed than the global average.*

*I didn't want to live my whole life that way, like a drone. With no hobbies besides studying and sleeping.*

I don't know, Hui . . .

I don't think you could have been like that. Because you played music.

*What?*

Didn't you play the guitar, in the story? And you said that you sang church music too. So you must have had some hobbies.

*. . . No.*

But that doesn't make any sense.

*Those activities—they weren't hobbies.*

*Music was just another stupid subject I was forced to study as a child. And I studied it really hard, actually. Way beyond singing in our bedroom.*

You mean you sang onstage?

*Not sang—performed. When I was the same age that you are here, our parents enrolled me in a conservatory for children. So that I could wear a white dress and play the piano in concert halls as a professional musician.*

But that's amazing! How long did you play the piano for?

*Eight years.*

That's a really long time. You're turning twenty-seven soon, aren't you?

*Yeah.*

So it was almost a third of your life.

. . . Why haven't you mentioned this about yourself before?

*It's not relevant, is it? By the time I moved to England for university, I had dropped all that music nonsense.*

You don't play at all now?

*No. I . . .*

*I would rather die.*

*Anyway, how did we fall into this weird rabbit hole about music?*

Well—

*I don't want to talk about it anymore! It's frivolous—and unrelated to my stories.*

But I'm curious!

*Too bad! Because I have literally nothing to say about that period of my life.*

Even though it was eight years long?

*Yes. It happened, and then it passed—that's all. It has absolutely nothing to do with who I am now.*

I highly doubt that.

*But it's true! That's why I never mention it to anyone outside this room.*

Not even Thomas?

*No. He knows I took piano lessons as a child. But not the extent of it—that I was a performer and everything.*

. . . Wow.

Could you tell me a story about those piano years, Hui?

*What? No!*

*No. Definitely not.*

But why?

*Because there's nothing to say! I told you already! Why do you keep pressuring me?*

*I don't know if you remember—but before we got sidetracked, I was actually on an important mission with these stories! Talking about big, salient, political themes.*

But I don't want to hear about those topics anymore.

*What? Why?*

Don't know. I've lost interest.

*. . . Are you fucking kidding me?*

No! I'd rather hear more about you, and what you went through—music, and studying, and feeling desperate to leave Singapore—

*But those topics aren't important!*

They are to me! Don't you remember what I said, before your first story?

I'm here in this room because I want to feel close to you again.

*And you can be! But only in the same way as with the last three stories—where I told you all about me as an adult. My social persona; my political outlook; my brightest and best takes on contemporary issues—*

That's all there is to you? All these big, important thoughts?

*Yes! Absolutely!*

Then you've lived a terribly small life.

*. . . What?*

*Hey! What did you say?*

*. . .*

*Say it again! I dare you. You think you can push me around?*

*But maybe you've forgotten—in this room, you're not my boss!
I'm the one in charge here—I'm the one narrating all these
stories, not you! And I don't have to do a single thing you ask
me to——*

Hui, don't shout.

I know you're only getting louder because you feel afraid.
Of what we might find if we talk about those piano years.

*I just . . . I don't want to disrupt all the work we've been doing
so far! Our stories in this room—they were going so well until
now!*

*You can't make me change course and talk about the past.*

That's true. But if you don't do it, I'll disappear.

*What?*

*But you know you can't leave this place!*

You know what I'm talking about. I'll still be here, but I'll go silent—look through you when you speak. Or switch off midway through your sentences.

You'll be invisible to me again. Exactly like with . . . well, you know who.

*Hey, hey now, there's no need to be so drastic—*

I'll do it, Hui. You know what this room is.

And you know how it works.

*Nin, I . . .*

. . .

*I can't do it.*

*All that stuff you want me to talk about—I really can't, okay? I can't tell that story.*

*So please, let it go! I have to do something else. I have to!*

. . .

*Nin?*

. . .

*Oh for fuck's sake! Nin?*

. . .

*You know what? Fuck this. Fuck you! You think that my entire world depends on you responding?*

. . .

*Well, you're wrong! Because I don't care if you ignore me like this—stay silent, then! Go on!*

*I don't even want to talk to you, anyway.*

. . .

*You think I'm pathetic, don't you? That I'll keep waiting around for you, like a dog . . . but I'll show you! I don't need you.*

*I can tell the best story yet without you!*

. . .

*And sure—I might have exhausted all the prime material from my life now, since it's only a "small life." According to you.*

*But just you watch—I'll find some other hot-button issue to talk about! And turn it into a three-act play with a giant bleeding heart . . . some issue like . . . gentrification? Or wealth inequality? Or . . . or the green movement under capitalism?*

. . .

*And I know what you're thinking—that it won't work because I don't know squat about those topics. Or even care that much about them . . . But so what? I could start caring, couldn't I?*

*Watch me! I can start right now!*

# HUI'S FOURTH STORY

## *The Green Place*

### I

SHORTLY AFTER QUITTING my job as a professional green-washer, I fly out to the Good Green Place.

That's the name I give it in my head, anyway, in the lead-up to me actually going to live there. Everything about this hostel in the Baltic region seems manifestly perfect—from the leafy, sun-drenched pictures of its forest compound to the promises that comprise its advertisement for volunteer staff. The ad paints a picture of an off-grid establishment whose owners are dedicated to creating a strong sense community and to subsisting sustainably, off of the resources from their land. They are looking for volunteers who'd like to learn and work via skill swapping, and experience eco-friendly tourism's future firsthand.

I first come across this advertisement on my laptop while holed up in my apartment in London. Outside my windows, summertime looms: the worst heatwave in a century is tearing through the city and calling a crisis of conscience into being. Climate change protests break out, attracting thousands of people—from Extinction Rebellion to school-aged climate strikers, everyone is leaping into the fray.

I, on the other hand, elect to stay at home. I barrel through my Facebook newsfeed for hours—surfacing occasionally in terror, short of breath. I can feel the facts spilling over in my head: two degrees Celsius of warming, thirty-seven billion tons of carbon dioxide. Eighteen months left to save the planet.

Picture me balled up in front of my laptop, teetering on the edge of a panic. Now picture me propelled by the frenzy of this moment to retch all the buzzwords that I can think of into a voluntourism forum: "eco-friendly," "intentional community," "sustainable."

The ad for the eco-hostel in the Baltic region pops up. I click on it like it's driftwood and I'm drowning.

*Look at this piece of heaven on earth*, I think, skimming too quickly through the website that appears. I marvel at the few pictures on display: tanned blond people with excellent posture, harvesting vegetables in the middle of a forest. They're greeting the sunrise with vinyasa yoga and carving furniture out of live-edge wood. They're posing in front of their eco-friendly sauna system, or crouched over on the soil, improvising a makeshift solar panel from scratch.

*Go there!* commands the anxiety that leaps into being inside me and dances around like a wicked flame. *Go there and start being part of the solution to this crisis.*

I locate some contact details and begin to draft a message to the hostel's proprietors, a husband-and-wife team: "Would it be possible for me to volunteer with you?" I want to learn new skills from their community, I write, so that I can take some practices back home with me to London and start living in a way that is better for the planet.

The hostel owners respond enthusiastically. They want to know how soon I can get there.

I axe all my social media tabs and book plane tickets. I beat the dust off my walking boots; I unearth my sixty-liter rucksack from storage.

And soon enough I'm sitting on a plane, hurtling off towards the Good Green Place.

. . .

BEFORE I WENT to live in the Good Green Place, I thought I was clear on what greenwashing entailed. For a number of years, after all, I had worked in a marketing consultancy, where clients sometimes badgered me to make their products look "greener." Even when these products were not actually green at all, but plainly—and sometimes virulently—bad for the environment.

*Why not wrap your logo in bramble?* I might suggest something like this to a bottled water company known for extracting from drought-stricken rivers. Or, hypothetically, to the makers of mass-polluting, palm oil–based products: *Have you tried incorporating green hues into your packaging? Or putting the words "Close to Nature" somewhere on your tins, since "Certified Organic" is legally out of reach?*

Over time, these experiences calcified into a belief for me: that greenwashing was something perpetrated by sleek and suited businessmen who wanted to extort money from know-nothing consumers in the city. London, I told myself, was a hotbed for this practice, given that it was crawling with greedy, soulless companies. People here wanted to seem green without enacting any reform. They wanted to seem progressive without sacrificing profit.

All day long, I sat in stuffy little rooms, schooling large corporations in borderline deception. But in the evenings as

I rode the Tube home, self-loathing questions would run on a loop through my head:

*Is this a job that you feel proud of doing?*

*Are you standing on the right side of history?*

*Why don't you walk away from this awful gig and reinvent yourself?*

It took me three years to find a way to leave my job. But as soon as I did, I was sure of what had to follow: I had to switch sides immediately and start playing for the good guys.

Which was why—I thought—I was flying all these kilometers, away to the light and space of an actual forest. Sitting on the plane and gazing out of its windows, I felt like a fresh lump of clay waiting to achieve form. I felt like I was finally ready to meet my newer, better self, under the guidance of eco-warriors who adhered to actual standards.

I was about to be surprised, in other words, by everything that happened once this plane touched down across the continent.

· · ·

TO GET TO the Good Green Place from the airport, I take a tram and then a bus. The two-hour bus journey winds beyond the city's outskirts and trundles along a forested path to the coast: the salty dark sky, the Baltic Sea. I sit next to a stony-faced grandma, counting down the minutes to arrival. *Finally*, I think, *I'm doing something that's good for the world.*

The hostel owner meets me at a nearby bus stop and loads me into the back of his van. He looks, at first glance, like everything I'd expected: masses of tangled blond hair, dirt-stained sandals. A fraying, ancient lumberjack shirt. He's the kind of person I would never have met in my previous life—poised on the front lines of change, while maybe wielding some sort of obscure woodsman's tool.

As we chat on the way back to the hostel, the owner doesn't ask about my ecological credentials, or why I'm here, or any of the topics that we've chatted about so extensively online. Instead, he only wants to talk about my capacity to perform labor. I've said that I'm not very interested in helping them with construction jobs, right? But I can still do other tasks?

"Sure," I say, as a memory of the hostel's ad flashes in my head, and I imagine all the exciting new skills that this place has to teach me. I wonder how I'll be of service to its cause.

When we disembark at the eco-hostel's grounds, I immediately feel hopeful. As advertised, this place is situated smack-bang in the middle of nowhere. And it looks like the kind of space where a non–climate striker could potentially reform herself: light filters greenly through the trees onto buildings twined artistically out of wood. Chickens run free in the backyard behind the kitchen; the overall environment smells vaguely bacterial. As I lug my rucksack around the compound to my tent, I call to mind the closest sensory reference that I can muster: the produce aisle of a Whole Foods in London.

It's at this point, while I'm imagining Whole Foods, that I almost stumble face-first into a hole right in front of me. "Fuck," I stutter, looking down in shock.

The hole in the ground is strewn with rubble and located at the edge of the compound. It's about a meter and a half across each way, and deep enough that I could have been injured. Concerned, I squat down to peer into its depths: there's an ugly neon-orange contraption nestled down there in the dirt, with thick black wires spewing from its frame.

"I see you've found our diesel generator," says the hostel owner, passing by.

The content of this sentence isn't what shocks me, so much as the nonchalance with which it's said. *Die-sel gen-er-a-tor*, I think, distending each syllable. It takes me a moment to make the connection: Diesel as in *that* diesel, the diesel that's annihilating the planet?

"Aren't you running your hostel on clean energy?" I demand.

"Not fully," says the hostel owner. They have a few solar panels sitting in the garden, but they need the extra power to keep this place going.

And how much diesel do they use?

"We turn it on nearly every night," he says, his voice trailing off along with his person as he vanishes into the distance. "I mean, we have to heat up, like, forty showers a day, or something . . ."

Still reeling from my discovery, I inch my way around the generator in the ground. On the other side of the hole, I locate the shared tents, which turn out to house twelve other volunteers. One of them is a woman from Argentina, who's leaving and whose spot in a shared tent I'm meant to be inheriting tonight. She's been here for a month, she informs me, while squashing her T-shirts down into her rucksack.

What a long time! I enthuse. She's probably learned all kinds of new skills from being here!

The woman from Argentina snorts. "What new skills?" she says. "You mean housework?"

"Let me give you a piece of advice," she says. "Whenever you catch a break in your volunteering schedule, try and grab one of the hostel's bikes and leave this place. Otherwise, they'll make you work non-stop."

"Good luck!" she concludes, as she runs the zipper straight across her rucksack and exits from the front of what is now my tent.

## II

BACK IN MY former marketing job, I tended to rely on a few key principles to identify when greenwashing might be afoot. One of these principles was that greenwashing, generally, tended to involve some degree of linguistic fuzziness. Like all storytellers, the greenwashers whom I worked for liked to play with words—pushing the limits of their usual plasticity, stretching and bending them to their will.

I saw this happen outside of my job too, in the more famous cases of greenwashing that came to public notice. Sometimes, brands would experiment with the negative space around language, to hide less-than-palatable facts from consumers. *We're carbon neutral*, an airline might gleefully crow, while choosing not to mention that their statistics were based on aspirational targets rather than actual results achieved. Other times, a brand might use imprecise terms that yielded whole spectrums of possible meaning. A global food manufacturer, for instance, might call its projects "sustainable," even though they caused large tracts of deforestation in West Africa. If challenged, this manufacturer might simply shrug its shoulders and wiggle its way around the vagueness of the term—*We meant "sustainable" as in "recyclable packaging," not "good for trees."*

By the middle of my first week at the eco-hostel, I'm starting to sense an interpretive looseness that reminds me, vaguely, of this particular aspect of my former job. I already suspect that language can be flexible here, since the hostel's purported eco-friendliness includes an unannounced diet of diesel. Still, I'm shocked the first time the hostel owner comes back from the supermarket with his van full of plasticky groceries for the guests.

"Aren't they trying to grow their own food?" I ask, gazing mournfully out across the compound at what I had previously assumed was its thriving veggie garden.

"Oh, they only grow, like, three things there," someone explains.

Likewise, despite the owners' supposed dedication to a strong sense of community, relationships in the hostel are far from ideal. Instead of pursuing cooperation and equality, the owners remind me of the worst kind of tyrants—constantly inventing new rules to intimidate their volunteers while hammering home their position of authority. "There's a food shortage," one of them announces to us, "so no more eating eggs from now on." But not even a few hours pass before the husband fries himself four large eggs in the kitchen.

On another memorable occasion, the owners accidentally overbook some guests. So in the wee hours of the morning, they bulldoze into the tent of two still-sleeping volunteers, causing them both to snort awake in terror. "We need this tent back," they declare. "Go sleep outside." When the two volunteers eventually burst into tears over this incident, the hostel owners try to remedy the situation by invoking the parental clincher: *Well, girls, remember who owns the roof over your heads!*

Ultimately, though, what upsets me most is how the hostel redefines its promise to facilitate skill swapping. Early on in my stay, the hostel proprietress arranges a meeting with me to discuss the subject.

"What do you want to learn from us?" she trills. A long-limbed golden girl who leads the hostel's yoga sessions, the hostel proprietress looks so healthy that she almost glows—as if she's starring in an ad for green juice.

I perk up. This is the moment that I flew all the way out to the middle of nowhere for! I want to learn about the hostel's specialized off-grid systems, I tell my host, like its DIY eco-friendly rain showers. Or its sauna roof, which seems, based on the description on the hostel's website, to be a natural structure—could I at least have a behind-the-scenes peek at its power and water supplies?

I want to strap in and learn the new skills that I was promised.

The proprietress's face takes on a visibly strained expression. Then she says, "Honestly, I don't know or care how all that stuff works. Why don't you talk to my husband about it if you really need to know?"

"So anyway," she goes on brightly, "how about I put you in charge of . . . washing the guests' dishes instead? That might be a good skill for you to learn too, right?"

Over the next few days, I wash so many dishes in the hostel's open-air kitchen that my hands turn red and half my face peels away in a sunburn. That, as it turns out, is pretty much all I ever get to do—six days a week, sometimes for up to four hours a day. The rest of the time, I wander around trying to redirect my questions to the hostel's other owner—who roundly ignores me, unless he's barking at me to perform some other variant of drudgery. *Sweep the floors! Wipe the tables!* None of these chores involve learning any new skills—let alone any expertise from the front lines of climate consciousness.

Suffice to say that by the end of week one, my confidence in the Good Green Place has deteriorated considerably. At night, while the diesel generator drones on, I lie awake in my mosquito-ridden tent and wonder: Have I been conned into flying out here? Into performing free labor for what is, essentially, a scam?

Maybe there were never any new skills on offer here at all. Maybe I should pack up and leave.

The mosquitoes circle me in the darkness of my tent, whining as they angle for blood.

• • •

PRACTICALLY SPEAKING, THE point of greenwashing is nearly always profit. This idea is even wired into the word's etymology, with its latter half—"washing"—referencing a story on the subject.

In 1983—this story goes—an environmentalist named Jay Westerveld was traveling in Fiji when he noticed a placard in a hotel. This placard implored travelers to please reuse their towels instead of relegating them to the laundry pile each day. In the hospitality business, it chided, too many guests were asking to have towels laundered that were only lightly used, wasting a massive amount of water. They ought to help save the earth's precious resources.

But instead of feeling inspired by this request, Westerveld got angry. This hotel, he theorized, didn't care about pursuing more impactful, but also more expensive, forms of activism—such as switching to a phosphate-free detergent that wouldn't clog or pollute the waterways. It was only keen to push for changes that would reduce its own costs—in this case, by reducing the number of laundry cycles that it had to pay for.

Westerveld decided to dub this form of behavior "greenwashing," in honor of the situation that had brought it to his notice. Greenwashers, he explained, didn't truly care about the environment and were only using it as a pretext. What they truly cared about was generating selfish profit for themselves.

Selfish profit turns out to be a topic of great interest during my second—and thankfully, final—week in the eco-hostel. It all begins one morning when a curious guest puts the hostel owner on the spot by asking him to explain his business model.

"Does this place close for the winter?" asks the guest, sidling over to the owner during the breakfast service.

"Of course," says the hostel owner, caught mid-bite. "This is only our summer gig."

But how do he and his wife spend the winter, then? Do they run another project like this one in a more temperate part of the continent?

Well—says the owner, sipping his coffee—usually they simply pack up after the summer months and go traveling for the rest of the year. "We make enough money because we don't pay for labor," he says convivially, nodding towards the kitchen where I am elbow-deep in soap-suds. He doesn't even bother to keep his voice down as he heartily declares: "Full-time work really isn't our thing. It sucks! I don't know how any sane person could stand it!"

I try my best to stay quiet in the kitchen, even as this new information dilates in my head and bursts apart in waves of fresh, frenzied outrage. *Oh my god*, I think. *My work here isn't helping the planet at all! It's just subsidizing the holidays of two absolute freeloaders!*

Later that evening, in my tent, I open the Instagram page of the hostel proprietress. I scroll through her most recent vacations with her husband: gorgeous beaches, breathtaking mountaintop views, city nightclubs and cobbled streets.

"Wow," says one of the other volunteers, when I show her this page. "They've been to more countries in the last six months than I've visited in my entire life."

From this moment on, it feels like a switch has been flipped in my head. I start to see the profit motive everywhere I look—lurking within each of the hostel owners' decisions and animating even their most apparently benign, eco-friendly actions. *Stop being so cheap!* I find myself fuming internally when they bemoan the length of guests' nightly showers. When they jabber on about how we need to care for the earth and keep using the filthy, wretched-looking sponges in the kitchen instead of buying new ones from the supermarket: *Stop trying to sell us on the language of greenness! I know that you only care about scrimping for yourselves.*

The final straw comes at the end of the week, when the hostel owner tries to justify why only he—and not the rest of us—ought to continue eating the hostel's eggs. Recognizing the displeasure that his recent ban has caused, he gathers all the volunteers to lay out some numbers: the hostel's hens, he tells us, produce fifteen eggs a day. And there are twice that many guests to feed. Technically, he could buy some extra eggs to feed us all—but only if he switches from buying organic to buying cheaper, battery-farmed ones.

"And is that what you all think we should do? Buy shitty eggs that are bad for the environment just so you can have some?"

Sitting in the middle of this beautiful sunlit compound in the forest, I close my eyes—and think of the hostel proprietress's Instagram feed. The roving backdrops of her many, many selfies. It's not that they can't afford to feed us, I decide. It's that they would rather not spend the pittance—and are happy to frame this stinginess as activism.

That afternoon, I conclude that enough is enough. I book myself a room in an ordinary hotel in the nearest big city, and fling all my clothes back into my rucksack. Once I've plowed through my last-ever mountain of dishes, I announce that I'm leaving early.

The hostel owners are totally unfazed. They don't even ask why I've changed my schedule.

The next day, I take the cross-country bus back to civilization.


## III


THERE IS SOMETIMES a kind of escapism, I think, tucked inside the eco-movement. Often, we're tempted to think that if we flee somewhere remote enough—tossing off the shackles of modern consumerism in exchange for pastoral bliss—then a bright veil of faultlessness will materialize all around us. Elsewhere, we kid ourselves, it's easier to make good choices—to avoid the compromises demanded of us by the strictures of our own normal lives. Society's habits keep tripping us up, you see, frustrating the very best of our intentions—we want to eat organic, but come up short at restaurants. Or we want to do planet-friendly jobs, but find ourselves selling out for income—rent, after all, is so damn expensive. It's impossible, we might lament, to live ethically where we are; the only real solution is to cut all ties, uproot ourselves, and start anew somewhere else.

*Go away from this place and live free*, purrs the whisper in our heads. This wishfulness is all around us, giving shape to our aspirations. It's in the teenager reading Thoreau's *Walden* in their suburban bedroom—and envisioning a rough-hewn, ascetic lifestyle on the fringes, in greater harmony with nature. It's in bougie think-pieces describing the utter impossibility of green living in the city—and remarking that the only real recourse, to achieve a state of complete moral purity, is to go off-grid in the forest.

It's me sitting in my flat in London, panicking about the environment, and then deciding that the best course of action is to fly clean across the continent, spewing 150 kilograms of carbon dioxide along the way. Believing that the solutions to this crisis must, obviously, reside elsewhere—in greener, leafier pastures somehow more conducive to virtue.

But what happens when this fantasy falls through? When we find out that hypocrisy has, all along, never had an address—has never been bound to one specific type of landscape or community?

In the months after coming back from the Good Green Place, I experience a jumble of emotions. The most immediate one has to do with shame—my embarrassment at having fallen victim to the tools of my ex-trade. *How was the trip?* friends ask. *Fine*, I answer, squirming in my seat while strategizing desperately to change the subject. *I should have known better*, I berate myself internally, wincing at my own memories; I should have smelled the greenwash from across the continent, instead of falling for it so clumsily.

But it's another emotional shift that takes me by surprise. After the shame recedes, a new feeling begins to stretch out inside me—until one afternoon, I find that it has emerged fully formed as a thought:

*Since the scammy eco-hostel wouldn't teach me anything useful, why don't I try to figure out this green-living thing for myself?*

Here, in London? The epicenter of capitalism in Europe?

Leagues and leagues away from anything resembling paradise?

*Why not?* I decide. *Why not at least try?*

That night, I sit myself down and google worm-composting bins for small flats. The next day, I take a deep breath and look up clean-energy suppliers in the city—realizing that, contrary to my expectations, several affordable options exist. Emboldened, I wait a few weeks and then read articles about buying better food—and finally, I cave in and join a few activist mailing lists. Start meeting other enthusiastic, bright-eyed residents of my own city.

*You did what?* these people say, when I tell them about my summer washing dishes in the hostel. *I could have taught you that,* they laugh, when I tell them why I went.

As it turns out, the Good Green Place is here, not there.

# ROOM

Do I have to say it?

*. . . What?*

That definitely wasn't your best story yet.

In fact, it was a bad story. Your first one so far.

*You're just upset because I started it without you.*

No—be honest, Hui. You know what I mean.

With the other stories, you might have slipped up by
mistake. Left details out, or fudged a few facts. But this was
the first time you tried to lie to me—on purpose.

*What are you talking about?*

You made up that last part, right? None of those life
changes happened.

*Of course they did!*

Then why did it feel like you were cooking them up?
As you rushed towards an ending—using grand words
like "we," "we," "we," and trying to wrap the story up
in a big shiny bow—

*I don't know what you mean!*

Don't you?

*No! I . . . I didn't lie.*

Okay. So—the worm-composting bins you said you
use now? Tell me something about them, then. Literally
anything—like, what brand are they?

*I don't—*

Or maybe you can tell me instead—what's the name of the
clean-energy supplier you've switched to?

*I can't . . .*

Or name me even one of the new activist friends you've
made, Hui!

. . . You can't do that either! Can you? Because there never
were any new friends!

*Okay, okay! Fine. I admit it.*

*I made up the last few anecdotes about becoming more
eco-friendly.*

But what made you think you could possibly get away with it?

You know who I am, and what this room is! You can't fool me in here.

*I just felt like the story . . . needed the lies, okay?*

*Because everything until that point was completely true! I really did go on the trip to that horrible eco-hostel. And if I couldn't say something, at the end, about how it changed my life, I'd have missed the whole point of those two awful weeks—*

Which was what?

*Oh my god—weren't you listening?*

*For me to start caring about the environment!*

Was that really why you went, though?

*Of course. I wanted to help the planet.*

Then why didn't you leave on the first day, when you saw their diesel generator?

*I . . .*

*I guess I didn't want to . . . act on a snap judgment . . .*

But after that, you stayed on through so many more red flags! When you learned that they didn't grow their food. When they wouldn't explain their off-grid systems to you—

*What are you saying, Nin?*

That I don't think you were there for the environment.
Even though you think you were.

. . . Because something else continued to keep you there,
right? Long after you realized that they couldn't teach you
anything?

*I . . . I'm not sure . . .*

Why did you really stay at that eco-hostel?

*I don't want to talk about this anymore.*

But this part is so important!

And what made you so upset that you had to run away from
them? I know it wasn't really because of their policy about
eggs. Or even because you cared about their greenwashing
at all—

*Oh my god!! Stop it!*

*I don't know, okay? There! I fucking said it.*

*I don't know why I stayed there, or why I left. Are you happy now?*

. . .

*After my last chat with you—about Singapore, about the
past—I felt like I needed to tell some story about that*

*hostel! And I really, truly thought that the point was the*
*environment . . . but maybe you're right! Maybe it wasn't.*

. . .

*And that's why the story sounded fake, right? Because I got my*
*own intentions wrong? That's why I needed to cap it off with*
*such obvious lies.*

. . .

*You're disappointed in me now, aren't you? You must be! And*
*I'm sorry that story failed, okay?*

*But I really was trying my best with it, you know—to force out*
*something that fit my mission in this room. About a place that*
*looked good on the outside, but was actually rotten—*

But why does that even matter, Hui? WHY?

WHY ARE YOU SO OBSESSED WITH THIS THEME?

*. . . I don't know.*

It's because you're rotten too, aren't you! Somewhere on the
inside, past all your perfect stories?

You're exactly like these places you keep saying you
hate—using something shiny to conceal the truth! And
that's why you had to pretend you went on your trip for
the planet—because you couldn't admit the real reason to
yourself.

*Nin, I . . .*

There was something else happening at the eco-hostel, wasn't there? Something bad.

That reminded you of your life from a long time ago.

*Nin . . .*

*I can't do this.*

What?

*I'm sorry. I just . . . I can't do this anymore.*

*I can't go on, with you pushing me like this! I'm so tired of it all—telling these stories, and especially that last one. So bad that it spoiled everything . . . my whole run in this stupid place . . .*

What are you saying?

*I think I want to leave this room.*

You mean you're giving up?

*. . . Yes.*

But what about me?

*I guess I have to leave you too. Since you can't come with me.*

Fine then. Go ahead.

Remember what I said earlier? You can leave any time you like. It's not like you've done it very much, over the years— but it is possible. There's always been a door.

*I remember. One that lets me go in and out.*

Will you ever come back to this room again, Hui?

*I honestly don't know.*

*Right now, I don't feel like I'll ever want to. I wish this room would disappear forever.*

Don't say that. You might change your mind.

Who knows. There might be a time when you feel like being here again. Or feel like you need me.

*I guess.*

Will you know how to find this place again, if that happens?

*Yes. Don't worry.*

*But will you still speak to me, the next time I come back?*

. . .

*Nin?*

. . .

*Please, Nin—*

Goodbye, Hui.

*. . . Goodbye.*

You know I can't answer your question. This room is your room.

But I love you. You'll always be my sister.

# YEARS TWO
# AND THREE

*The Depths*

WHAT DID WE TALK ABOUT IN OUR VERY FIRST STORIES, when we were children? When we were together in that dark little bedroom of ours, so many years ago?

In one of the stories we were cats, I remember. In another we were squirrels. We lived in houses; we lived in trees; we leapt across the glittering rooftops of cities. Sometimes we remained sisters in the stories we acted out; sometimes we turned into friends or neighbors. Always, though, something monstrous was coming for us, and I was teaching you how to bear it. *It's here now—be strong*, I'd instruct you, in the voice of a smaller, frightened creature.

The point was that you were young, back then—or at least younger than I was. Too young to tell the stories yourself, but not too young to listen. So every night, you let me talk and talk—until what was happening to me each day, outside the room, took on the form of a story. Became weightless and lifted off my mind, so I could live to endure another day.

When you wrap something bad in a story, it becomes possible to bear. Words can do that, you see—protect you, by making the ugly seem beautiful.

But you already know that, don't you?

You know exactly what I mean.

It's been so many years that I've forgotten what it was we had to bury. What was it that kept happening to me, that I had to hide away in words? Now that we're in the room again, anything is possible—the stars are wheeling overhead and time is swimming in reverse. The night is congealing all around us now; our shared mattress is hard under our backs. The fan is spinning, slowly, slowly. The air still smells of eucalyptus oil.

You're here beside me, once again—will you always be here? Hold my hand; we're moving backwards this time. Talking our way down through the layers of story until we reach the truth.

# ROOM

Hui!

*Hey.*

You came back! It's nice to see you.

*You too. I wasn't sure if we'd be able to go back to talking.*

But you know how this place works.

*Well, sometimes I forget.*

*. . . Can't believe six months have passed since I was last here.*

Is that so? I can't tell in here.

*I know. It still surprises me, after all these years—how time never affects this room.*

*The fan, the darkness, the humidity, even the crickets . . . everything is the same here! Even though so much has changed for me outside.*

Like what?

*I guess the biggest change is that I moved back to Singapore from London.*

Interesting. Did Thomas move too?

*Oh—no. He stayed behind.*

*That . . . wasn't a mutual decision, actually.*

What do you mean?

*Well, you know how bad our marriage was getting. The shouting, the violence, that one time I pulled a knife . . .*

I remember.

*So a few weeks after I left this room, I flew back to Singapore for a holiday, to visit Mum and Dad. But while I was there, Thomas called me and said he wanted to take a break from our marriage.*

Oh, wow.

*Yeah. He used the word "divorce." And of course, I panicked. But then he explained that he was only considering it, not demanding one.*

*He said he needed space to decide. So he asked me not to come back to London, since I had already quit my job to work remotely.*

Gosh, Hui. I'm so sorry.

That must have been terrible for you to hear.

> *It was—it was unbearable. To feel like I'd finally fucked it all up for good.*

How did you cope?

> *Well, for the first few weeks, I didn't. I cried—uncontrollably.*

> *But now that a couple more months have passed . . . I don't feel so devastated anymore.*

Really? You're not worried about the future?

> *Of course I am! I mean—soon I could be twenty-seven and divorced.*

> *But maybe it's better that we're living separately now, to give each other space. And on top of that . . .*

What? You trailed off.

> *Well, there's something about living in our parents' house— and being back in Singapore—that also feels . . . right for me, somehow. Even though I know that by most people's measures, it's a downgrade.*

You feel like you need to be there, and not in London?

> *Exactly. Come to think of it, the feeling appeared right after I left this room—I had this overwhelming urge to go back and see their house.*

The place where you grew up.

*Yeah.*

Even though you were once so desperate to leave it?

*I know . . . isn't that weird?*

*So anyway—here I am. Back on the equator again. Living in our empty childhood bedroom. And to be honest, almost every day I wonder if I've made the right choice.*

Why?

*Because I don't know what I'm looking for in our parents' house. Most of the time, it feels like I'm just waiting for a sign.*

It might be that you'll know it when you see it.

*I guess.*

*Actually, Nin, there's been one other big change in my life. I should tell you now, before I lose my nerve.*

What? Why do you look so shifty?

*I've started talking to somebody else besides you.*

Oh. I see.

*But it's not because I don't like you anymore!*

Well, who is this person?

> *She's a grown-up. And she listens to me talk for fifty minutes a week, while I lie down in a dark, quiet room.*

She's basically replaced me, then. You tell her stories about your life too?

> *You could say that. I mean, she's a professional listener, with a lot of analysis techniques—she understands how people's minds work.*

So she gets what you're doing with your stories.

I mean, what can I say, Hui? This person sounds good. It'll probably help you to see her.

> *I hope you don't mind, though! I didn't want you to feel hurt.*

You know that's not something I have a choice about, in this room.

> *. . . That's true.*

But why did you come back here then? If you have this other person now?

> *Because we have unfinished business, don't we? I never managed to tell you that last story properly.*

Oh.

You mean the one about the eco-hòstel?

*Yes—do you remember it? With the fake-sounding ending, where I told you a bunch of lies on purpose?*

Of course I remember. I remember everything you tell me here.

*If I gave that story another go, would you be willing to listen?*

. . . How truthful can you be this time?

*Honestly, I'm not sure. I don't know if I fully understand what that situation was about yet. Those weeks in the forest . . . hating everything and everyone . . .*

*But I have had six more months to reflect. So maybe I can tell it a little differently now.*

No more deliberate lies.

*No. I want to at least . . . try. To find out what really went on there.*

Okay then.

Give it a shot—I'm listening.

# STORY FOUR AGAIN

## *The Green Place*

THAT SUMMER, IT felt like the world was on fire. A gash in the universe had opened above us, and a thick wall of heat came streaming down: soaking over our skin, seeping into the tarmac. Pulsating in waves through the clear city skies, so that they glimmered with all the malevolence of an omen.

*Climate catastrophe*, shrieked the news reports each morning. *Take heed, humanity. Mend your ways.*

Instead, I packed myself a rucksack and tried to escape— over the continent from London to a country on the Baltic coast. I was going to live on the outer edges of a forest, with some strangers I had met on an internet forum.

These strangers—a husband-and-wife team—ran a business that they referred to as an "eco-hostel." Practically, what this meant was that they owned a stretch of land where they entertained paying guests during the summer months. Housed in tall white yurts, these guests spent the daytime roaming about the hostel's vicinity—wandering through the shifting patches of sunshine in the forest, or cycling to the cusp of the Baltic Sea. Afterwards, when they returned to the eco-hostel for dinner, a large log fire would be waiting for them in welcome.

I found out about the eco-hostel's existence via an online advertisement, beckoning me to join its community. The ad explained a form of barter trade in which volunteers, like me, could supply the hostel with several hours of manual labor each day. In exchange, the hostel would give us—what? My attention skimmed across the bulk of the text and homed in on a few key promises: opportunities to learn about how to subsist off the grid and to swap skills with the hosts; the warmth of a close-knit community; a chance to partake in eco-friendly tourism's future.

Three tiers of benefits, worth the high asking price of my labor, time, and travel. Maybe, as a volunteer, I'd acquire some handy green-living skills from these people. Or maybe I'd find myself nourished by new relationships, which would set me on a better path. Or maybe—and this was the most tantalizing fantasy of all—I'd return home newly hopeful about the future. Hope was in such short supply that long, broiling summer. Who even knew what a person could still expect, as they watched the world rock back on its axis and then plummet towards calamity?

*Eco-friendly tourism's future.*

I liked that idea. I polished it in my mind.

## I. SUBSISTING OFF-GRID; SWAPPING SKILLS

AT FIRST GLANCE, the eco-hostel looked like an environment highly conducive to learning.

By this, I mean that it looked unlike any place I'd ever seen before—I, who had spent most of my life thus far revolving between cityscapes, parsing different expressions of concrete and glass. This eco-hostel was the opposite of concrete. It looked like someone had plucked an image from a fairy tale and deposited it in the heart of the forest to put down roots—and to blossom into an open-air yoga studio, a kitchen in the sun, and hammocks that stretched out lazily between the trees. To sprout a hodgepodge of picnic tables, which circled a bustling chicken coop—and off to one side, an outdoor spa system devised out of a chain of bathtubs.

Everything was either upcycled or made out of live-edge wood. Standing at the hostel's periphery and gazing across its compound, I wondered what new forms of eco-consciousness I was going to be learning here: Permaculture? Timber repair? How to run a business on clean energy?

This last illusion, at least, died almost as soon as I had imagined it. En route to the volunteers' tents to deposit my rucksack, I tripped and nearly fell into a large crater—which, upon closer inspection, housed a hulking neon-orange contraption with thick wires spewing wildly from its frame.

"Our diesel generator," said the hostel owner, when asked about this object.

Diesel—as in traditional dirty energy? How much of the hostel's power were they sourcing from the machine?

"We turn it on nearly every night," came his airy reply. "You'll hear it buzzing near your tent, unfortunately."

Okay, so improving my understanding of clean energy was probably off the table then. Never mind. There'd be other skills to learn.

The next morning, still feeling fairly buoyant, I met with the hostel proprietress. She took me through a long account of all the housework I'd have to perform to earn my keep there, including but not limited to: sweeping floors, scrubbing dishes, cleaning the compost toilets, and playing receptionist to the hostel's many guests. "Let me know if you have any questions," she concluded at the end of this whopping inventory.

I did, I exclaimed, seizing the opening. I had so many questions to ask her about the off-grid systems that sustained this place—the ones that had been gushed about so ardently, yet vaguely, on the hostel's website. Could I learn about its DIY eco-friendly rain showers? Or about the natural roof of the sauna? How about its specialized electricity and water supply systems—I couldn't wait to get an up-close-and-personal tour of how it all worked!

The hostel proprietress blinked at me with a strained expression. Then she reconfigured her facial muscles and said, "Uh . . . I mean . . . sure?"

"But honestly," she continued, "I don't know or care how all that stuff works. Why don't you talk to my husband about it if you really need to know?"

What was going on? I wondered, slumping away dejectedly from our meeting. Wasn't being off-grid the entire point of this hostel in the forest? So how could it be that this woman, the co-owner of the place, didn't have a clue how the systems worked? Also, why did she seem so stunned by my expectation that I'd be learning about them—why else did she think I had flown out to this boring place in the middle of nowhere, prepared to slog through a thirty-hour workweek for two strangers on the internet?

Over the next few days, I did my best to waylay her husband and redirect my long list of questions to him. I'd try to approach him cautiously as he bustled behind the trees, wielding his chainsaw in terrifying fits of raw energy. Shirt off, he seemed to be constantly working on some new project or other—building waterbeds for the guests, repairing a faulty oven, or pulverizing felled trees down to usable firewood. "What do you want?" he'd snap, each time I approached. "Can't you see I'm busy? Ask me later!"

Soon I gave up on getting any information from him. Instead, I resigned myself to knowing so little about how to get by off-grid that, to my chagrin, I couldn't even explain the basics to the hostel's guests. *How come the rain-showers here only run hot at night?* fascinated guests kept asking me, as I showed them to their yurts.

*I think that they need the daytime hours to . . . heat up in the sun?* Left without a single piece of real knowledge to fall back on, I'd find myself peddling obvious, low-quality errata. Once, the hostel owner happened to be doing some repairs within earshot as I delivered one of my self-devised presentations to a group of guests. After the guests had oohed and aahed and trooped off to their yurts, I turned to him in the hope that he would verify— or otherwise, dispute—my claims. Much like the guests, I was dying to know: How did the hostel's systems actually work?

A nasty smirk unfurled over the owner's face. "Honestly," he said, "it doesn't matter what you make up. The city-folk who come here will believe any old shit you say."

So I never did uncover the truth about the hostel's showers. Likewise, my hopes of learning about sustainable food production died a quick and brutal death once I realized that the hostel bought most of its food from a cheap supermarket nearby. Plastic-wrapped cheese; cans of tomatoes; crinkly bags of carrots. "We simply don't have the capacity to grow our own stuff," said the hostel proprietress when I expressed my disappointment.

They didn't have a nice, lush permaculture plot for me to tend to, then? Or, say, a large-scale composting project that I could try my hand at?

"Nope," said the proprietress, not looking up from her MacBook. "You can water the plants behind our chicken coop if you get really bored."

Suffice to say that by the end of week one, it had become abundantly clear that I wouldn't be learning any new skills for off-grid subsistence here. Nights after work, as the generator droned on toxically outside my tent, I'd lie awake trying to sort out my thoughts: What was going on here? And more to the point, had I been tricked? Why did it feel like I was performing an endless mountain of chores, without gaining any new knowledge in return?

## II. A CLOSE-KNIT COMMUNITY

BY THE MIDDLE of my second week, I was thoroughly unhappy. I had decided that apart from teaching me zero new skills, this eco-hostel was becoming an increasingly hostile social environment.

There were eleven other volunteers working alongside me. For the most part they were nice enough, hailing from different countries and covering a broad age range, from youth to middle age. Several were university students, a few were yoga teachers, and one was a theater professional from Berlin. One night, while the theater professional and I were doing our laundry in tandem, I mentioned that on the flight out here, I'd been listening to a spoken-word album by my favorite artist, Laurie Anderson.

"Oh, her," said the woman as she scrubbed her underwear. "She's great in person. We had drinks together once when she and Lou Reed were in Berlin."

Outside of this place, all of the volunteers appeared to lead rich and vibrant lives in which they were valued, accomplished, and respected by other people. So why did they consent to receiving such terrible treatment here? I couldn't understand why everyone tolerated the levels of bullying.

Because bullying was what it felt like. Day after day, I watched the hostel owners push around full-grown adults who had flown here, from around the world, to offer them free labor—but who were now washing the dishes too clumsily, or folding the laundry too slowly, or making the meals a tad differently than instructed. "Useless," the hostel proprietress snapped at a medical student from the Basque Country, physically shoving the woman's hands away from the guests' breakfast preparations. "What's the point of you being here if I have to do it all myself?"

Her husband was even more unpleasant—at least to me. On my very first morning of work in the compound, I made the mistake of asking him if there was a different, stiffer broom that I could use to sweep out the layers of dust caked on the hostel's floor. This was enough for him to stalk over to me, saying: "I have no respect for lazy people who blame their tools."

He kept coming closer until his glare hovered almost directly over my shocked face.

"You are the problem here," he hissed. "*Not* my broom."

The unhappiness caused by these incidents aside, there was also the matter of the owners' arbitrary decrees. Far from the utopic, non-hierarchical mindset I'd expected, the two of them seemed to find great joy in limiting other people's freedoms and reminding us who was in charge over and over. *No more borrowing the hostel's bikes until Tuesday*, they'd suddenly declare—effectively stranding us in the middle of nowhere, more than an hour's walk from the nearest small town. On another memorable occasion, they overbooked some guests, then realized their mistake in the wee hours of the morning. So they barged into the tent of two still-sleeping volunteers and shook them by the shoulders until they snorted awake in terror.

"We need this tent back now," they informed them. "Go sleep outside."

After word of this incident got round—both volunteers having cried, publicly, in its wake—the hostel owners attempted to justify themselves by invoking the age-old parental clincher: *Well, girls, remember who owns the roof over your heads!*

The language of community made one other notable—and equally unpleasant—reappearance at the start of the second week, when the hostel owners decided that there was a food shortage. Eggs, they declared, would now be an item reserved only for guests. "We're a family here, and family eats last," one of them intoned, trying to gaze with meaningful intent around our group.

None of the other volunteers made a sound of protest—even as over the course of the next few days, we all witnessed the hostel owner brazenly whip up several omelets for himself.

But tensions finally came to a head one night when we gathered to eat our usual workers' dinner in a circle, sprawled on the floor of the outdoor yoga studio. The hostel owner waltzed over to the group, smiling. He approached one volunteer, an Australian woman, and held out his hand: in it lay a single brown egg still cold from the fridge.

"Naomi was very good today," he said, to the group. "Tell everyone what you did to earn your egg today, Naomi." He stooped down very low—towards this former marketing executive who was almost forty years old, and who had come here in an attempt to recover from the corporate grind. He looked like he was about to reach out and pat this adult woman on the head.

The woman began to attempt a response—but then gave up, and just smiled weakly around the circle.

Why would any self-respecting adult let themselves be patronized like this? No matter how I spun the situation around in my head, I couldn't figure it out—all the other volunteers seemed like brave, decisive people. So why weren't any of them trying to leave? After all, none of us were contractually beholden to this place none of us were even a little bit obliged to be here, suffering through this.

What could everyone possibly be getting out of staying?

Whenever I was able to talk to the other volunteers offsite, I would try to steer our conversations towards these questions. In our spare time outside of work—the owners' injunctions notwithstanding—we'd grab whatever bikes we could from the hostel's shared stable and speed off into the forest before we were stopped.

*Don't you think that the hostel owners are . . . kind of . . . horrible?* I'd ask while we rode.

The replies never varied.

*Totally. They're way more demanding and selfish than other hosts I've met on this forum.*

"They've changed," one returned volunteer explained, looking sad. "They were so much less awful two years ago, when I last worked here."

The Basque medical student and her girlfriend burst out laughing at my question as we cycled together to a nearby beach.

"They're one hundred percent assholes," one of them said, wiping her eyes. "Actually, within the hostel, the two of us have code names for them; we call them the 'King' and 'Queen' in our language, so that we can complain about them without others understanding."

Replies of this sort would always flip a switch inside me. I'd feel the blue heat of vindication shoot right up my spine and crackle ferociously in the base of my skull. *You know what?* I'd announce, *I hate those assholes too! I'm thinking of leaving early—even if I have to walk the eight kilometers with all my damn luggage back to the bus stop!*

*Would you like to join me?*

But for some unfathomable reason, the other volunteers always expressed great reluctance at this prospect. *Well,* they'd say, *it's true—the owners are unpleasant. But we've only got a week left in this place, and it seems such a shame to let go of it all . . .*

As they spoke, their gaze would always begin to expand and float upwards, as if it were being drawn into the ether. Squinting in confusion, I'd try to follow their line of sight, which always seemed to be trained in the direction of nothing. Some trees; the sunshine. The bright blue sky. In the Basque couple's case, they held hands and looked towards the open water, where literally nothing of interest was happening at the moment.

Finally, I decided that enough was enough. I was tired of being belittled and criticized; of sweating through rote work for no discernible gain. Coming to this eco-hostel had been a total waste of time. I booked myself an ordinary hotel room in the nearest big city. Then I threw all my clothes back into my rucksack and announced my early departure.

The hostel proprietors were totally unmoved. But some of the other volunteers swapped contacts with me. "Sorry that the people here got too much for you," said one. "But at least you got to experience all the rest of it, right?" She leaned in for a hug.

Except for the rare, brief moments of letting off steam with the other volunteers, I couldn't think of a single facet of this experience I'd enjoyed.

The next day, I took an early bus to my new hotel.


### III. ECO-FRIENDLY TOURISM'S FUTURE


IN HIS 1979 book *Distinction*, the sociologist Pierre Bourdieu laid out a concept called the "habitus." Some elements of a person's early social environment—this theory goes—are wont to sneak into their body in ways that are automatic, and that lie beyond the realm of deliberate control. In their gastronomic tastes, for instance, or the particularities of their walk. In their preferred style of leaning against a doorway, or scooping their body up from an armchair; in the pitch of the laugh that they might use to impress someone.

The underlying structures of a person's social life are ingrained into their very musculature, says Bourdieu—like a fine pattern only visible in certain slants of light. Their social background is there all the time, in the dips and swells of their body's responses—in the thousand tiny ways that body might seek to adjust itself in order to wring maximum benefits from the world around it.

The point is that bodies never really stop playing by the rules of their most familiar environments—even if they relocate to different countries, or up or down a social ladder. They stay true to the priorities and beliefs that they once absorbed from their earliest, most formative surroundings—and then turned into their own brisk forms of carnal intelligence.

For a long time after I came back from the eco-hostel, I struggled to articulate what had disturbed me so deeply about the place. Initially, my stories leant heavily on the word "scam"— as in the spitting declaration, *That whole hellhole was a scam.* The hostel owners, I'd tell people, had made me work such long hours! Which would have been fine if there had also been some sort of reward for all my efforts: some new skill to learn, or some infusion of human warmth.

But this place had delivered neither. It had simply been flat-out awful.

But something about this explanation would always give me pause. Even as I delivered it, I could tell: too many unanswered questions crested under the smooth skin of its narrative. If the place had been a complete rip-off, then why did none of the other volunteers get as angry as I did? Why did no one else want to leave? If I was being totally, brutally honest with myself, some of them had even seemed vaguely . . . happy to be there.

Over several months, I told and retold this story. I repeated it to anyone who gave the faintest sign that they might listen, barreling through all the details I could remember: the characters whom I'd met, their words and misdeeds. I'd twist it all into a narrative that was also, at its heart, a question: What had really happened to me out there, in that terrible hostel on the coast? I was desperate to find a good-enough answer.

It was a long time before one of my listeners finally ended my search. "You've talked so much about this place," a friend complained, after I told him my story for what might have been the ninth or tenth time. "But I can't picture it at all, because you never mention what kind of nature there was."

Leaning back in his chair, my friend squinted at me. "This hostel—it was presumably in some kind of forested area, right? What kind of trees did you say there were, again?"

I sat very quietly, trying to remember. What had the forest all around the eco-hostel looked like? What sort of trees had there been, lining that particular lip of the Baltic coast—tall ones? Short ones? Coniferous or deciduous? I strained to remember literally anything about them at all—their smell, or the sounds that they made. I kept coming up empty.

And what about the ocean, that day when the Basque couple and I sat by it and talked about leaving—what had it felt like? Warm or cold? Was it even an ocean? Or had it been some kind of freshwater lake?

I reached back, in shock, through the clear fluid of my memory. Holding my breath as I tunneled on and on.

I realized that I couldn't produce a single convincing answer. My mind had retained every aspect of the eco-hostel that had been built by humans. It remembered the shapes of all the buildings with absolute precision. And it remembered the people most clearly of all—their emotions, their exact words, the tiniest shifts in their facial expressions.

But its reserves didn't contain a single usable memory of trees.

The whole time I'd been in the forest, I hadn't noticed the natural world around me at all.

. . .

LET ME TELL you something about the concept of the habitus, as it applies to me.

I grew up in a city in the dead center of the world. A sleek, edgeless, pearlescent city, sparkling with fluorescent lights and manufactured sounds. A long time ago, this city was a jungle. But now it's a place that recycles its own wastewater for drinking—subjecting it to molecular engineering and ultraviolet lights in the pursuit of better-than-nature quality.

In the city of my childhood, the trees that we care about most are the ones in our multimillion-dollar SuperPark—fifty meters tall and sculpted out of concrete, then covered in a glinting layer of steel. At night, these artificial trees glow from within, broadcasting the blue-green fires of mechanical life. The proof of humanity's dominance and nature's subservience. The proof of our ability to make and remake the world.

There are other trees in this city too, of course: ordinary, organic trees subject to the usual ignominies. But these trees we reserve for functional purposes only—using them to fringe our roads or border our shopping malls. As sources of shade, or as markers for the sites where a person might exercise. If the trees don't serve these functions well, then our government immediately cuts them down and paves them over with something more practical—like a condo or a new expressway. After all, nature has to earn its keep. Has to earn its spot on our crowded little island, where every living being is fighting for its own tiny portion of soil and space.

In the city where I grew up, there was little credit to be had for coexisting peacefully with other forms of life. For noticing nature's existence and then leaving it be. Once I became an adult and left, I sought out other cities that were organized around similar principles—big, angry crucibles of man-made energy. I knew that I would always be more comfortable there, in places where nature remained no more than a resource—grist for the mill of human activity, or else redundant and out of sight.

But how have these environments shaped my body? What have my eyes and ears grown capable of perceiving? The truth is that my heart beats fastest for concrete—for steel. For shopping malls, when I travel past them in the heat of the afternoon sun, imagining all the variants of human exchange that must be happening within them. When I feel emotional and want to be around water, I don't seek out the sea, or rivers, or even rain. Instead, I go to the public swimming pool to pickle myself in chlorine, do quiet laps, and cry into my goggles.

My eyes light up for the urban skyline. My body knows all the particularities of the city in a way that, I suspect, it will never get to know any forest anywhere on earth. In a way that involves total projection into the landscape; that involves relinquishing all the bland details of its selfhood to wide, immersive possibility.

Maybe the concept of habitus means that, essentially, you cannot choose. You cannot choose what catches your breath—or conversely, what might evade your notice.

At the eco-hostel, I walked into a forest for almost two weeks and emerged entirely unmoved by the natural landscape that had surrounded me there. Its textures and intricacies slid off the surface of my mind, even as the other volunteers soaked it all in: the sky, the sea, the shades of green. The bike rides and the long, hot walks in the sun. The crispness of the breeze; the crunch of gravel underfoot. That must have been why they stayed, I realized, so many months afterwards. Why they endured so much criticism for so long, content to glean almost nothing in the way of new skills.

They stayed for the natural world, which seemed blank to me. Which never seemed like enough of a reward on its own.

Their bodies were attuned to the benefits of the place in a way that mine couldn't be.

. . .

FUNNILY ENOUGH, ECO-FRIENDLY tourism's actual future ends up confounding all expectations. Half a year after my time at the eco-hostel, the COVID-19 pandemic grinds travel to a halt. Flights get canceled or turned around in midair; hotel chains shut down; social media influencers remove the multiple flag emojis from their bios. The atmosphere clears.

By then, I've moved from London back to Singapore, the city of my childhood—the city so intent on subjugating nature. But now, with months of lockdown in place, activity in the city thins to a trickle: the shopping malls empty and the swimming pools close. The SuperPark shuts off its light-up trees and closes its doors, utterly deserted.

People leave their homes for food and the only other form of outdoor activity permitted by the government—walking around in nature for exercise.

On a humid evening, as the sun sets, I take a walk around my parents' neighborhood. I turn a corner that I've never seen before—and find, at the end of the asphalt that lines the space between houses, a row of striped posts. A bright red sign nestled in the grass.

A bright red sign that means: *Here ends the city. Here ends the known universe. There is nothing past here that is worth your notice.*

I step past the sign.

On the other side, the grass comes to my ankles. When I've walked a little further, it comes to my knees, then my waist. The land gradually rises in a broad, uneven slope—and then tunnels right down to a trench of dry leaves, like a moat.

In the center of the moat: tropical flesh. Huge ferns drowning out limbs of dark and glossy wood, vines looping over and under and hanging down in swirls as they climb up, up, up towards the last rays of the sun.

Trees. Not lining or fringing or providing shade; not doing anything besides standing in the way of the light like a last green lick of fire.

What trees are these? Somewhere in this city that once was a jungle, someone must still know their true names.

I take a deep breath.

I reach out my hand so that flesh meets flesh.

# ROOM

You did it, Hui! You tried to tell the truth.

*As much of it as I could recognize, anyway.*

I noticed that this time, you didn't mention the greenwashing at your previous job.

*I know! Six months ago, I couldn't stop obsessing about that aspect of the work.*

But now it doesn't bother you?

*Not as much.*

*In fact, I wonder if the first story exaggerated how bad the work got. Because sometimes, I did have to teach companies how to look more eco-friendly. But that certainly wasn't central to the job—or what upset me most about it.*

What upset you, then?

*. . . It's hard to explain this.*

*But near the end of my time at that place, I started to get this terrible . . . fear. Every time I clocked in and sat down on my swivel chair.*

What were you afraid of?

*That I'd never be able to leave.*

Really?

*Yeah. All these visions would multiply in my head—of me growing old and dying there. Trapped in that small, cluttered room at the top of a walk-up, earning next to nothing. And laboring away over PowerPoint slides that felt meaningless to me . . .*

But why couldn't you just quit?

*The company was sponsoring my visa to live in England.*

Wait—what?

I thought you said Thomas was your sponsor! In the story from last year.

*He was, eventually.*

*But actually, this company sponsored my visa for almost three years first. Right after university.*

You never mentioned that.

*Well, it's like you said, right? Sometimes I slipped and left details out, when they made me feel rotten.*

*I'm trying not to do that anymore.*

Good, Hui. Because that's how you'll find it.

*"It"?*

What you're in this room to remember.

*I'm not sure I—*

So anyway, tell me more about marrying Thomas.

Was that your escape plan from your job?

*Yes. And we rushed through it frantically for that reason— didn't plan a wedding, only focused on the paperwork.*

*I was terrified the company would find out and jump in to stop us.*

Could they even do that?

*I don't know! But I felt it in my bones—that if they could, they'd trap me. So I'd never be able to walk out the door and find a better life.*

And yet marrying Thomas didn't take that feeling away from you.

*What do you mean?*

You felt trapped again in the marriage, right? Once you were depending on him for a visa?

. . . I could feel it when you were telling your story last year. Describing how the marriage was limiting you, and forcing you to live on Thomas's terms.

*That's true.*

*I did feel trapped.*

Was that why you ran away to the eco-hostel, after the marriage?

*I guess so. I was very insistent that Thomas shouldn't come.*

*I thought going there would make me feel free again.*

Only it didn't.

*No! Not at all! In fact, I felt at my worst out there, in that middle-of-nowhere hellhole. That I couldn't leave without a car, or at least the borrowed bikes—*

You emphasized the bikes more in this version of the story.

*I did?*

Yeah. Especially how the owners would withhold them, on a whim.

*I hated that! How they made it so obvious that we were at their mercy—helpless to leave the hostel grounds without their permission.*

It almost sounds like they were holding you captive.

*It felt that way, you know! Like they had physically trapped me.*

You weren't only being held back by a concept, like marriage, anymore.

*No. Now the trap was literal. And it made me feel desperate— especially because we were so isolated, far away from anyone who could help—*

Well, it's good that you managed to leave them early!

*Only by one day, though.*

. . . What?

*Wasn't that in the story?*

No. I assumed you quit much earlier!

*Oh. Well, I didn't.*

*I'm sorry—I didn't mean to hide that information from you.*

I wonder why it didn't cross your mind to mention it, though.

*Maybe I felt embarrassed.*

*There was no reason why it should have been so hard for me to get up and leave that shitty place, right? I don't know why I stayed on for so many days—even after they'd humiliated me, and I'd seen their generator in the ground . . .*

There was no contract, was there? Saying you had to stay?

*No. But even then, I somehow couldn't bring myself to leave.*

*You know, it took all my strength to even manage that escape of one day! To engineer it all—booking my bus tickets and new hotel on the sly, without drawing the owners' attention—*

In case they jumped in to stop you? So you couldn't walk out the door?

. . . You know, it sounds a lot like what you said about your ex-company. You seem to feel this way a lot.

*It's almost like the feeling . . . follows me around.*

From your job, to your marriage. And then to this forest.

*Yes. And even when I run from one place, I still feel trapped in the next. Like I'm . . . imprisoned by someone.*

*So that I have no choice but to do whatever it is they want— whether that's make PowerPoint slides, or adapt to life in Europe, or wash dishes in the sun.*

And it feels bad for you.

*Yeah! Like I stop being a real person and turn into this . . . puppet. A doll—or a character—in someone else's story. Who can't leave, or voice their true thoughts, or act on their desires—*

I understand that feeling very well.

*You do?*

Yes—in this room, at least.

It's not easy, is it? Feeling powerless like that?

*No! It's the worst feeling in the world!*

*And I've carried it all my life.*

. . . Hui, there's something else I've been meaning to ask you.

*What is it?*

You know how your body couldn't see the trees at the hostel? Is that the only thing your body can't do?

*What do you mean?*

Well, I was thinking about how it never comes into this room. Can it not do that, either?

*Wait a minute—what do you mean, my body never comes into this room?*

*It's here right now! Can't you see it?*

I can see *a* body. But I'm sure it's not your real one.

*. . . What?*

This is a kid's body, Hui. You're aware of that, aren't you?

*Of course! But I thought that was one of the rules of this room, or something. Because I always look this way here.*

Like your eight-year-old self?

*Yeah! It's been like this ever since I started coming here. Are you saying it could be different?*

I'm pretty sure you could look any way you wanted to here.

*Like my adult self, even? With a twenty-seven-year-old body?*

Yeah. Isn't it strange how you've never tried that?

*I mean . . . even thinking about doing it now . . . makes me feel uncomfortable.*

That's not surprising. It's not like you ever mention your adult body in your stories, either.

*I don't?*

No. You talk a lot about what's happening in your head, but never about how you look! I don't know if the body you currently have, outside this room, is tall or short. Or skinny or fat . . . or what your face looks like—

*You're kidding.*

No! In all the years you've been coming here, you've never once described your face. You didn't even describe it in that last story, when you were feeling all emotional.

*. . . Damn.*

*I guess I really didn't.*

*I wonder why, though. Because it's not like I'm trying to keep my adult body a secret on purpose.*

Maybe you don't like it much.

*That can't be true. Outside this room, I've done a lot of wild and empowering activities with it.*

Like what?

*Partying—substances? Stuff like that. And clubs too, where adults can get hurt or humiliated for fun.*

*My body has done a lot that I shouldn't talk about, Nin, given how young you are here.*

And it feels good, doing it?

*Well, no. But my body feels—something.*

*Which is more than what it's used to.*

So it's used to feeling nothing?

*Nin . . .*

*Do you still remember my story from last year, about being depressed?*

Of course.

*So the thing is, my body often feels kind of detached from me. It's always doing these actions I can't control—like crying, or lying down, or turning into a stone.*

*But when I'm wasted or experiencing pain in clubs—in those moments, my body works. Even if what it's working on is the act of disappearing, to survive.*

I'm sad to hear that.

*Why?*

It's sad that your body only works when you're hurting it like that.

*Do you think something might be . . . wrong with it?*

*Because even at the hostel, I couldn't get it to do what I wanted. Everyone else was swimming in lakes, or going on hikes, but I couldn't.*

Like your body couldn't enjoy those activities?

> *Yeah. I couldn't even go cycling that much—only a few times, to complain with the other volunteers. Mostly I lay around in the shared tent.*

Ew! That doesn't sound comfortable at all.

> *It wasn't. The air inside was boiling, and it stank of everyone's sweat . . . but I couldn't get up. So I just lay there on the foam mat and browsed the internet. Or wrote long, angry iPhone notes about hating the place and feeling trapped.*

> *What's wrong with me, Nin? I'm a mess, right? Completely rotten—*

Hui, when you were little, did anything bad ever happen to your body?

> *. . . What?*

> *What do you mean by "bad"?*

Just anything difficult . . . or even strange . . . that you can recall.

> *Well, you know how I have that memory gap. So maybe I'm missing something.*

> *But I know that the year I turned sixteen, I had spinal surgery.*

What for?

*Scoliosis. The top half of my spine was curving outwards to the right—by eighty degrees. It almost crushed my lungs.*

That sounds terrible!

*Oh, it wasn't that bad. It was two weeks of lying in bed to recover, tops. And then I could walk again.*

But what gave you the scoliosis?

*I don't know. Part of it was genetic.*

*But the doctors did always say it was strange—someone as short as me shouldn't have had the condition so severely.*

Maybe something happened to worsen it, in the years before.

*I don't think so! I mean, I wasn't doing anything then . . . only living my usual life, and going to school—*

And playing the piano a lot.

*Yes. That too.*

*But it was all boring. The stuff that I've forgotten.*

Have you forgotten all the details of your surgery too?

*. . . Huh!*

*Actually, I haven't.*

So your memory gap ends there?

*Yes! I never noticed it before—but in fact, I can remember the exact beige of the hospital ward's walls. And the disinfectant smell, and the sounds from the corridor outside: the beeping, the rattling. Somebody crying. And the heaviness of the new titanium rods in my spine.*

*I can even remember the dreams I had while sleeping in the ward.*

But the years before that moment?

*I can't see them in my mind.*

I wonder if your body can remember them, though.

*What do you mean?*

Maybe your body knows what happened in those years.

And that's why it's so tired, you know? From always holding in the secret.

*You're saying that my body isn't useless and depressed for no reason.*

*It's—*

Waiting, I reckon. Until it can talk to you.

. . . Have you ever tried asking your body to tell you a story about those years?

*No! What would that even look like?*

I don't know.

*Well, I don't know either.*

Maybe I should go quiet for a while, so you can figure it out.

*What?*

*Please don't do that! You've seen what happens, how I spiral when you're silent—*

But from now on, there will be realizations you have to arrive at this way, Hui.

*Without you?*

Yes. And the silence might feel terrible, if you fill it with your fears. But if you don't, it could take you to new places. Surprising ones.

You already know that, though.

*But—*

Let's try it once, okay?

If it feels bad, we can stop.

. . . *Okay then.*

. . .

*Nin?*

. . .

*Right. We're really doing this. Only me . . . and all my thoughts.*

. . .

*How to ask my body for a story?*

*I don't know.*

*Last year, when you first wanted a story, you said you wanted to be close to me again, right? I remember that.*

. . .

*And I guess that outside this room, I've been doing something to be close to my body too. Along with the psychoanalysis sessions. Maybe it's worth mentioning.*

. . .

*I feel weird bringing it up, though. Because it's a bit . . . unusual. I feel like it's the kind of activity other people might judge me for.*

*But you said not to think about my fears, right? That's the only way to get through this silence.*

. . .

*I've actually been doing these pencil drawings of my naked body.*

*I do a few each week. And I'm not an artist, so the sketches are probably quite ugly. But they're also making me feel . . . curious. I don't know why exactly.*

. . .

*I draw my face and hands the most. But the other day, I drew my legs too, all the way to my genitals.*

*And tracing the exact lines, trying not to exaggerate or beautify, leaving in the folds and spots, even the wrinkles I'm ashamed of . . .*

. . .

*Sometimes when I do these sketches, it feels like my body is . . . trying to talk. Trying to be honest with me.*

See? That wasn't so bad!

You worked something out.

*It doesn't feel like it.*

Why not?

*Because I don't know if these sketches are the answer.*

*Doing them feels important. But I've been making them for what—almost three months now? And it's not like anything new has happened.*

Your body still hasn't told you its secret?

*No. And to be honest, I wonder if it ever will.*

*Maybe it's hopeless.*

Or maybe something important is missing from your drawing exercise.

*Like what?*

A key! For turning your body's voice from pictures into words.

*What could that be, though?*

That's a good question.

. . . You know what, Hui, why don't you tell me another story?

*But what about the missing key?*

That's what the story is for. To give us some ideas—instead of us puzzling away in the dark like this.

*I guess it's worth a shot.*

*I should warn you, though—at the moment, I'm in a pretty bad headspace for telling stories. I'm still living in our parents' house. And the whole of Singapore is under* COVID *lockdown.*

So you're trapped in their house all day?

*. . . Yeah.*

That sucks.

*I know. The storytelling part of me feels stifled. Restless.*

*Like a teenager again.*

Hm . . .

When you were an actual teenager, you were desperate to leave their house, right?

*Very much so.*

Tell me a story about that, then! About your first time leaving.

*Okay. Let me see . . .*

*. . . So the year I turned nineteen, I ran away from our parents' house to do a work-exchange program abroad.*

After you finished school?

*Yeah—for three months. In the gap between the end of school and the start of university.*

Where did you go?

*To Jerusalem.*

That's so far away! I can't believe Mum and Dad supported you going.

*They didn't. But I was prepared—for a whole year, I'd saved my own money in secret so I wouldn't need their permission.*

*I was ecstatic when I managed to pull it off! I simply bought the plane tickets and announced that I was going—even though it enraged them.*

Why didn't they try to stop you in other ways, though?

*Like what?*

With physical actions, instead of finances. Like in the past, with . . .

*. . . What?*

Never mind.

Let's not get into that yet. What's important is that this trip meant a lot to you—because it was your first big encounter with that feeling.

*What feeling?*

Of escaping. And walking out the door.

*I guess.*

It sounds like it'll make a good story!

*You think so?*

Yeah! And telling it might distract you. Give you something else to do while we ponder how to help your body talk.

*Okay then. I'm ready.*

I'm listening.

# HUI'S FIFTH STORY

## *The True Wonders of the Holy Land*

### I
### LARA

LARA WANTS TO show me a picture of her fiancé. "Look," she giggles, dangling a hot-pink smartphone in front of my face. Her pre-wedding portrait looms into view. "Handsome, right? Quite tall? You like his suit?"

The man in the photo is totally nondescript. But Lara herself looks like a supermodel, with layer upon layer of white lace accentuating her silhouette. I'm sure that's why she showed me this photo in the first place.

Back home, I could never have hung out with someone like Lara, with her acrylic nails, skin-tight jeans, and rhinestone-studded everything. Her high-octane boy craziness totally unmarred by decency. When we met in the convent's back kitchen one week ago—soiled aprons wrapped around our waists, our elbows buried in soap-suds—the very first question Lara asked me was: "Do you have a boyfriend at home in Singafora?"

"Yes," I lied.

She narrowed her eyes. "How serious?"

"Me—I am engaged," she added almost immediately afterwards.

That winter, there was a definite hierarchy among the Palestinian teenagers working at the convent. At fifteen, Lara was the youngest—but she was also the reigning princess on account of her good figure and precocious matrimonial coup. In this kitchen in the Arab Quarter of the Old City of Jerusalem, Lara was the most glamorous person scrubbing the fossilized gunk off pilgrims' dinner plates. Swinging her hips to the boisterous dance music that blared out of someone's cellphone in the background.

What was I even doing here, washing plates with them? Lara was confused. She was working for the convent so she would have more pocket money after high school. But I was a volunteer who had signed on to do this for no discernable reward—other than the use of a spare bedroom in the convent's guesthouse for pilgrims touring biblical sites. "You flew all the way here from the Far East . . . to stack our plates?"

"Also to see the wonders of the Holy Land," I said.

"*Habibti*!" Lara snorted. "If I had three months of free time, I would take a real holiday."

On the days when we weren't working, Lara would invite me to her house in the Mount of Olives. There, we'd forgo spending time in the beautiful, world-famous Garden of Gethsemane in favor of admiring touched-up photographs in which Lara herself looked particularly attractive. Enthusiasm mounting, Lara would teach me how to tweeze my eyebrows to suit my face shape—an oval face, she explained, presented its own distinct opportunities and challenges.

At Lara's house I ate from the never-ending flow of snacks that her mom prepared, ranked Arab celebrities by body and face, and slouched against various soft furnishings as I rested my brain. Sometimes, though, I could feel all the things that we didn't want to talk about amassing and churning under the surface. Lara's marriage was happening soon, in months—which meant that her parents would be taking her out of high school. *When I'm older, I want to live in Europe or America*, she'd say. Her mouth would hang open as she gazed into the mirror, swabbing on huge gobs of under-eye concealer.

## ZEINA

I BECAME PROPER friends with Zeina on the day that I tried to visit the All-Important Church.

The All-Important Church was located a ten minutes' walk away from the convent whose dishes I was washing. It was so important to everyone because it was the holiest site in all of Christendom—six different Christian orders, in fact, shared joint custody of the place, bickering and squabbling over which relics belonged to whom.

All in all, the All-Important Church contained several specimens of All-Important Stones: a stone on which Christ's dead body was said to have been washed and anointed, post-crucifixion; some stones that marked the great bonanza discovery of Christ's probable tomb; and a stone where the history-making, world-changing angel most likely perched in order to break the news of Christ's resurrection to his mourners.

In the dimness of the church, I took all the photos that I could manage. Afterwards, exiting the building, I squinted at my camera; in the weak half-light of Jerusalem's midwinter, all the All-Important Stones looked exactly the same.

In my family's evangelical church back home in Singapore, I was the leader of a Bible study group. I went to service every Sunday and swayed to four-chord songs about the attributes of God. I liked it when ordinary things snuck up behind me and smashed a sense of rapture into my skull; I was gravely disappointed, in other words, to find that none of the special stones had affected me.

Lactic acid accumulated unpleasantly in my thighs as I walked back uphill to the convent. In the kitchen, a skinny teenage girl with long bleached hair was stealing slices of cheese out of the nuns' communal fridge. She then thrust them into the microwave, where they melted over a huge wedge of peppered meat. The smell of grease in the kitchen was overwhelming and, quite frankly, disgusting.

"Hi," said Zeina. Her cheekbones sliced like a pair of insults. "You must be the Singafora volunteer."

Zeina thought that Lara was hot, but dumb for getting married so young. "I don't know why all the others are so impressed," she complained, chewing her hunk of cheese-slathered meat. She herself was single, but moving onwards and upwards to better things—she was studying something to do with computers at Bethlehem University, in the West Bank. "It's more important to be smart than pretty!" she declared. She raised one oily finger and gesticulated forcefully at the ceiling.

Over the months that we washed dishes together, Zeina taught me a whole host of useful Arabic profanities. "Shout this at him," she'd command whenever I came in late for work with a story about some lowlife catcaller who had tailed me through the souk again. "They pick on you because you look fair and small," she explained. "Learn how to defend yourself, okay, little girl?"

Once, Zeina herself was late for work. "Checkpoint!" she shouted to the nuns, sweeping into the kitchen three hours later than scheduled. A torrent of Arabic streamed between her and the other teenagers as they slammed dirty cutlery back and forth across the counters. "It's okay," she said later, waving away my questions. "Sometimes it just happens."

## NIDAL

IN THE INTRICATE social ecosystem of the convent's labor force, Nidal played a role that I recognized: the guy who was suspiciously old to be hanging out with teenagers. "I think he's almost thirty," Zeina whispered. At this point, we were both nineteen. Thirty felt like the tail-end of mortality.

Despite being weirdly ancient for this work, Nidal was easy to love—a man-bear who lumbered into the convent in stained, rumpled sweatpants and bellowed out hearty greetings to everyone present. He cracked dumb jokes in which he himself was the punchline, and walked around with huge bags of the pilgrims' laundry balanced on his shoulders. He once tried to rap in English so badly—and with so much fervor—that even the older staff in the convent had to laugh. "*Halas!*" they shrieked, swatting him away and turning back piously to their floor-cleaning or reception-desk duties.

"What's Singafora like?" Nidal kept badgering me. "Better than here? Worse?"

"Watch out!" he joked. "Next year I'm going there to visit you!" We both knew that this was basically impossible. But at least Nidal had the blue ID card that let him travel through Jerusalem, instead of the green one that kept other Palestinians trapped in the West Bank.

Sometime in my second month at the convent, the nuns organized a big day trip out to Tiberias. They rammed all the foreign volunteers into one rickety minivan and whisked us off to various sites of great significance, such as the Messiah's Hometown and the Messiah's Local Synagogue. And the Messiah's Local Freshwater Lake—which was, confusingly, referred to as a sea in the New Testaments of our Bibles.

Each time we started off for someplace new, one of the other volunteers would read out a devotional text that they had penned under the Lord's own influence. They were all intrepid retirees who wore cargo pants, quoted Josephus fluently, and genuinely enjoyed parsing hermeneutics with the nuns. I, on the other hand, was falling asleep. I was also becoming progressively nauseated in the back of this airless, lawlessly speeding vehicle.

By the time we got back to the convent that evening, I was two hairpin turns away from a collapse. "Why so sad?" Nidal inquired as I stumbled in.

"My friend, I will cheer you up!" he continued, booming. "Tomorrow you can come to my house, and I will buy you hookah from the souk. You like apple flavor, correct?"

That Nidal had retained this piece of trivia about my tobacco preferences was as surprising as it was sweet. "Correct," I said. Then I went to my room to throw up.

# RAMZI

ONE EVENING DURING my final month in the Holy Land, Ramzi whipped out a key from the back pocket of his jeans. That night after work, he declared, we were all going upstairs to the convent's fifth-floor terrace. A rooftop view of the Old City! Rich tourists paid a premium for this shit.

Ramzi popped the collars of all his polo shirts with a confidence that bordered on contempt. He wore a gold chain and immaculate white skinny jeans, and had a high-fade haircut as sculpted as a work of art. He also had a Facebook profile that claimed he played midfielder for Real Madrid C.F.

"You know them?" he asked me out of the corner of his mouth, while expertly lighting two cigarettes at once. He inhaled from both sticks a few times before palming one off to Nidal.

"Not really. No."

"That's okay since you're a girl."

From the convent's rooftop, I could see the Old City sprawled out before me: magnificent, moldering, pockmarked ruin. Holy old chunks of spirit-sapping limestone. I was in a particularly foul mood that day because I'd spent an hour running around the souk trying to get into the Third Holiest Site in Islam. One of the convent's nuns had assured me that the place would be open from mid-afternoon onwards. But when I arrived at the most obvious entrance, a man with an assault rifle slung over his shoulder barked: "Muslims only! Muslims only!"

It made sense that he was being strict. After all, fanatics of all stripes in this city harbored ill intent towards the Third Holiest Site in Islam. Some wanted to build their Third Temple on its grounds—and made sure that everyone else in the

Old City knew it by marching down the streets at least once a month while bashing percussion instruments and screaming indecipherably. Other people—like the ones who went to my church back home—also wanted the Third Temple to materialize. But they were hoping for an additional, even more exciting epilogue to the drama, one in which Jesus came back to rule the world.

I only wanted to take a decent photo. So I circled the area, eyed the guards, and scowled at every person they let through the gates. I sat down in a fit of pique on a stone post, then bawled passive-aggressively on the phone to a friend—until an annoyed passerby told me to go around the block and queue at the special tourists' entrance.

Ramzi laughed in my face when I told him this story. "That's so stupid," he said. "You can see it from here."

He was right. Across from us, the golden dome of the Third Holiest Site in Islam was winking like a big, round taunt in the night.

Near the edge of the terrace, Lara and Zeina were squawking with escalating energy at some sort of choppy home video that was playing on WhatsApp. Nidal was cracking jokes with the other Palestinian part-timers while picking scraps off an outrageously large plate of food that someone had annexed for him from the pilgrims' dinner service.

The moon was bright. The air was cool. And the music being played was—defying all belief—even trashier than the usual Top 40 dregs we washed dishes to. Whenever a new song came on, Nidal would belt out the first line off-key while everyone else play-heckled his attempts. "*Aywa aywa!*" they'd briefly yell before talking over him again.

Ramzi conveyed my stupidity to the rest in Arabic. Screeching ensued. He looked down at me, grinned, and took an enormous, kingly drag off his cigarette.

"Next time," he advised me, "take it easy."

He blew out a stream of smoke. "Just stay here. We are the best attraction in Jerusalem anyway."


## II


ACCORDING TO THE *Holman Illustrated Bible Dictionary*, a wonder is fundamentally different from a sign. A religious sign, typically, contravenes some basic law of nature—as in water becoming wine, or a dead man defying entropy to pop back up to life.

But a religious wonder is different. It doesn't have to spark incredulity or defy belief in any way. All it has to be is marvelous to behold: a source of endless and genuine amazement. A wonder functions to turn your gaze. Or even, for a second, stop your heart. It whisks your breath away as it lifts off the visible surface of the world and crashes through your mind like a wave.

Ultimately, a wonder is capable of holding your attention because it is a conduit—a space of possibility that the spirit passes through. It hums itself alive with the raw energy of the divine. It looks straight back at you as you turn to contemplate its form.

The *Bible Dictionary* puts this distinction more succinctly: "Whereas a sign appeals to the understanding," it explains, "a wonder appeals to the imagination."

After I returned from Jerusalem, two separate developments occurred. The first, more predictable one was that I jettisoned my faith. Over a few months, I stopped going to my Zionist-leaning evangelical church in Singapore. I stopped reading the scriptures and stopped leading a Bible study group. Eventually, I stopped believing in Christianity's God.

The second development was much more surprising to me. One day, apropos of nothing, I sat down at my laptop and began to write. Prior to this point, I'd never attempted to write fiction before. But after I came back from the Holy Land, a deluge of imaginative work began to pour out of my fingers starring characters so wholly formed, they felt alive.

To be fair, these stories never featured any of the Palestinian teenagers directly. But more often than not, I found myself building new characters out of aspects of their personalities that I remembered. My characters had Ramzi's high-tops and Nidal's belly-laugh. Or spoke in Zeina's serrated voice, which sawed its way out of her chest to scale the walls of whatever room she was in. They kept tiny bottles of apricot-scented lotion in their purses, like Lara did. Or flipped their long, carefully conditioned hair in a perfect imitation of her.

I never tried to publish these stories. In fact, I never showed them to anyone. Instead, I would produce them in quiet, fervid bursts—then hastily flip my laptop shut again, as if to hold in the words. In telling stories, I found, I could relive my time with my friends—make the precise textures of their language and behavior come rushing back to me, crackling with electric energy on the page.

As the years went on, I forgot nearly every detail of the holy sites that I had visited. The assorted relics of the Holy Land stayed dumb and dead in pictures on my camera—or else gone to seed in the musty corners of the internet where I'd posted them.

But the teenagers stayed alive, as vivid as they had been all those years ago. I remembered every last detail about them— so much so that, sometimes, the feeling of their presence in the room would floor me. Turn my gaze. Or briefly stop my heart. Whisk the living breath out of me as I sat down at my desk to write about, and remember, them.

Ramzi had been right. They'd been the true wonders.

## III

IN THE SUMMER of 2014, three years after I returned from the Holy Land—and after Palestinians had experienced at least sixty-six years of apartheid and dispossession under the Israeli state, including forty-seven years of military occupation— operatives of Hamas kidnapped and killed three Jewish teenagers in the West Bank. Shortly thereafter, Israel's military invaded the Gaza Strip. In the span of seven weeks, it launched air strikes and ground invasions that killed up to 2,300 people and wounded over 11,000 more. Almost 500,000 people were displaced; around 1,000 children were left permanently disabled; 203 mosques were razed; nearly 150,000 homes were damaged, and more than 12,000 were completely destroyed.

On the Israeli side, five civilians were killed by retaliatory violence. And one more died from a heart attack while running to a shelter.

Outrage surged through the Palestinian stronghold of East Jerusalem. When Jewish extremists kidnapped a local Palestinian teenager at the start of the Gaza invasion—then doused him in petrol and burned him alive—thousands of demonstrators showed up for his funeral. By the end of the year, a whole rush of new protest-attacks had erupted, with newspapers murmuring about a Third Intifada. People were hitting back with sniper fire and knives, through vehicle attacks, or by lobbing stones and firecrackers. One person shot a right-wing Jewish activist point-blank, minutes after he delivered a speech about forcibly taking back the Third Holiest Site in Islam.

By early November, thirty-three civilians had been injured by these attacks from Palestinians.

But alongside this, Israeli military forces had injured a further 1,333 Palestinian people in East Jerusalem—among them eighty children.

By this time, I was living far away, watching it all unfold on the news. Then one day, out of nowhere, I received my first-ever email from Sister Erica—the tiny, sprightly nun who had been in charge of the convent's volunteer program all those years ago.

Her update implored ex-volunteers to offer prayers for Jerusalem. These were extremely troubling times, she wrote. The convent was now using its bomb shelter regularly, for the first time since the 1973 Yom Kippur War. The nuns were mostly fleeing for the safety of their homes in Europe or North America. They couldn't be sure when, if ever, cir-cumstances would improve.

I typed out their names in the order that their faces blinked into my mind: Lara, Zeina, Nidal, and Ramzi. "What about these people?" I asked Sister Erica. "My friends, who used to work for you. Do you know if they are safe?"

I never found out. Sister Erica never replied.

# ROOM

You're crying, Hui.

*It's the ending of that story. Remembering it again.*

*Sorry for making our mattress wet.*

Don't be. Maybe it's a good thing.

It's the first time I've seen you cry in this room.

*Really?*

Yeah. I reckon you used to do it more, long ago—when you
first started coming to a place like this one. But that was
before my time.

. . . Hui?

*Yes?*

Does it always help you to tell stories about people when
you lose them?

*What do you mean?*

You know—like how you wrote those stories about your Palestinian friends, after you'd fallen out of touch.

Or like what we're doing here.

*With me and you?*

Yes. Why do you always put lost people into your stories?

*I guess . . . it helps me to cope with the sadness of missing someone.*

*Because even if I can't see them, or talk to them anymore, I know I can bring them back to me with words.*

Move them around in your head.

*Exactly. So we can feel close.*

Have you ever thought about doing that with your body?

*What do you mean?*

Well, you said that you feel distant from it, right? And you're struggling to hear its voice.

*Yeah . . .*

So why don't you trick yourself, like with the teenagers from Jerusalem? Turn your body into a character in a story—so that it can talk.

*You think that's the key we've been looking for?*

Maybe!

*. . . I wonder.*

*There could be something to it. What you're saying—it actually reminds me of a story I read recently.*

Outside this room?

*Yes. Well—it was really just the opening paragraph of a much longer story. But in it, the author, Catherine Ragsdale, spoke about her body in third person for a bit. And*

And what?

What are you thinking?

*That it was kind of magical when she did that. Almost like she had cast a spell to turn her body into its own separate person.*

With its own feelings?

*Yes, and its own actions too. Independent thoughts that it kept trying to tell her throughout the day.*

So her body had a voice.

*I suppose so.*

That's what we're looking for! We should try following her approach.

*Okay. It feels kind of silly though, like messing around with language.*

Let's try it anyway.

How did her story start?

*I think it opened with the phrase: "Steadfast body."*

I like that.

*Me too. It sounds right.*

Because your body would be a heroic character if it were in a story?

*No, not heroic. More like . . . loyal. Unswerving.*

*I feel like my body—it'd be the kind of friend who'd never abandon you. No matter what you did. Even though they remembered everything that had ever passed between you—*

Like all the ways you'd hurt them.

*Yes. Or failed them.*

So like a sister, then.

Oh, Hui—don't be sad. I'm sorry I brought that up.

*I'm not sure I want to do this anymore.*

But we're getting so close now! Please don't give up.

Tell me more about this Body character. What was it like, as a child?

*Well . . .*

*It was soft and small, I guess. And constantly sweaty. Because it lived in a tropical, humid country on the equator called Singapore.*

And tell me more about its appearance.

*Why, though? You can see how it looks in this room.*

Tell me anyway. It's important that you turn the picture into words.

*Okay . . .*

*So . . . Body had a big tummy and a mushroom haircut. A bright, round face for grinning or scowling . . . and its favorite dress was red, I think.*

What did it do when it wore that dress?

*Race in a circle in its parents' garden. Or bounce on a big gym ball that its parents kept at home.*

Body sounds so energetic!

*It was! You know, for many years, Body was such a lively little thing—I remember that quite clearly. How at that age, Body was always moving: running around and playing games and shouting and chewing and laughing, until one day . . .*

What?

*One day . . . Body turned eight. And then all the movement stopped.*

Why?

*Because Body entered the conservatory to play the piano.*

*And then Body, it . . .*

*It . . .*

*Nin, do you hear that sound? That . . . low rumble. From outside the room.*

*. . .*

*What is it? It's getting louder.*

*Almost . . . expanding now, into a full roar. And now rising, rising in pitch—piercing, like a scream . . .*

*Wh—what's happening? Why is the room spinning?*

*. . .*

*Please Nin, answer me! What is this sound??*

*It's so loud now! And ugly, like one continuous rip through my head—like the noise an animal makes when it's fighting to live . . .*

*Oh my god. I know what it is.*

*This is my body's voice, isn't it?*

*. . .*

*I recognize it—from a long time ago. It's the sound of panicked flesh.*

*And I can hear words now too, deep inside the shrieking . . . it sounds like even more of them might be coming . . .*

. . .

*Please Nin! Say something—please!*

*Your silence—it worked, okay? I figured it out! But you said that if it feels bad, we can stop—*

It's okay, Hui, I'm here.

Hold my hand. There—can you feel it, in the dark?

*I'm scared!*

Don't be.

*But I can't bear to acknowledge these words—*

Your body's memories?

*Yes. Everything it's saying now. That it's starting to remember, from the years of the memory gap.*

Help your body to form the words into a story.

*I can't!*

*I can't even imagine a world where that would be possible—*

But you know you have to do it.

This is the story you've been searching for. It's what I woke you to find, right at the beginning. And it's why you've

stayed on with me, in this room, for the past two and a half
years.

. . . *Please don't let me face this story alone.*

You're never alone, Hui. Not in this room, anyway.

Tell it when you're ready. And take as long as you need—
you know how time moves differently here.

# THE STORY OF BODY

## I

"STEADFAST BODY." VESSEL and scribe of my afflictions. The channel through which all my intentions must pass; the only part of me that's fully seen. Small, lonely Body turning in its bed. Running like a breath of wind through its dreams.

Body of too many, too-vivid effluents. Unending need. Unfading memories. My body is trying its best to swallow a story, but the story keeps getting stuck in its throat. Why won't it go down? *Help me*, says Body, in animal language. Looking around the room with wide, glazed eyes. *Somebody help me. Somebody, please.*

## II

BODY'S PARENTS ONLY want the best. This is important to remember, going forward: Body's parents are ordinary, good-and-bad people. Like most parents, they actively want to benefit their child. They care inordinately for Body's more visible counterpart: Mind.

That Mind should be more visible than Body is somewhat surprising. After all, at this age, Body is always on the outside doing things: sweating and farting and running and laughing, and chewing and shouting and bouncing on a gym ball. But this is Singapore in the '90s: a country where, for a new generation of children, Mind has been touted as the key to success. The perfect—and by extension, perfectible—mind is an ideal held by many parents here. Prep schools start from age two and go up from there.

This country has one of the world's harshest education systems, and also some of its unhappiest children. By the new millennium, parents here will collectively spend over $1 billion a year on tuition. Suicide will be the leading cause of death for young people.

Here, the prevailing philosophy is: Every child must be stretched to their limit, so that no drop of potential is wasted. Every parent wants to give their child a niche, to launch them ahead in the endless competition.

The year that Body turns eight, Body's parents decide that its special niche is going to be competitive piano. Body has inherited a keen sense of beauty from its mother, and a bursting creative energy from its father. In early life, it has shown great enthusiasm for this instrument: whenever its hands encounter a keyboard, they sing, merrily, up and down the scales. Music fills its whole flesh with joy.

Body's parents take this joy for an inroad. They decide to send Body to a local conservatory that is known for the extremes to which it pushes young minds. Said young minds are so violently pushed that they often achieve adult qualifications long before puberty. But the cost of securing these results is notoriously difficult for young bodies to bear. Two to three hours of piano training each day. Multiple lessons to practice per week and lengthy theory sessions on the weekends. All of which must come on top of ordinary school.

Body's parents know the conservatory's reputation. But they are two young people with such great hopes. They want so badly for their child to achieve.

So they say to Body: *Let's go shopping.* And Body, with excitement, agrees. Body and its parents go out to a fancy shop and buy a piano that weighs eighteen times Body's own weight. Back home, they install the piano in a small, dark room, which is covered in thick and dusty curtains.

These curtains prevent sunlight from entering the home studio and warping the piano's wood. But they also mean that no one can look in and see what is about to happen to Body.

What happens is that Body, at eight years old, sits down on the piano stool.

And Body's joy ends.

Over the next year, and the next year, and the next, what happens in the piano studio is too terrible for words. And anyway, it is not the focus of Body's story, since Body can no longer recall it as a set of discrete, describable actions. But the main thing is that Body, which once was so happy, soon lives in a state of inexpressible fear. Each day, it fears the arrival of four o'clock, when its schoolwork is done and it will have to go into the studio for a length of time. When it comes out again, the sky is always dark. Body has always missed the sunset. Body fears the confines of that curtained, dusty room that it is not allowed to exit unless someone gives it express permission to. And most of all, it fears the demands that are being made of it within the room—demands that Body often has no power to fulfill, because it is only so little, after all. It is only the body of a child.

What happens to Body in this room, every day, involves a small group of adults. Some of these adults Body has lost contact with. Body has no wish to ever see them again. And anyway, these are not the difficult relationships. The difficult relationships are the ones with people whom Body still loves to this day: a mother who is always in the studio, threatening to inflict great cruelty and violence if Body does not continuously perform. A father who, by contrast, distances himself, claiming that he cannot bear to witness what is happening to Body: Body's loud sobs; its captors' screams. But this also means that he is never around to save Body when Body most needs him to do so.

Body's parents—as previously stated—are essentially good, kind, and loving people. But even good people can do bad things. They can bring such pain upon the bodies that they love. Upon the bodies that hold all their hopes.

Sometimes, when Body is locked in the room, it feels so depleted that it thinks: *I will never get out of here.*

Sometimes, when the pain gets especially bad, Body wonders: *Will I die here?*

Body doesn't know the answer to this question. It only knows that if it cries, or trembles, or slumps, or says no, the pain that it experiences escalates dramatically. Body soon learns not to cry. Body soon learns not to slump. Body soon forgets the feeling of "no"—the way that specific word once tasted in its mouth.

Body just sits still on the piano stool. It stops asking for rest and play. It stops wishing that it was somewhere else.

Body just tries to survive.

.  .  .

SEVERAL YEARS OF childhood pass. Then one day, when Body is eleven, something inside it snaps. By this time, Mind has progressed at the promised pace and is nationally ranked as a piano player. It seems to be en route to a promising career. But Body cannot take it anymore. So one day—after an incident where it chokes on some chicken at the dinner table—Body makes a unilateral decision. Henceforth, it will refuse to eat. Specifically, it will refuse to carry out the one action that involves rolling food into a ball with its tongue and guiding it backwards towards its gullet. *Maybe if I have no strength*, thinks Body, *I will not have to perform anymore.* The physical feats being asked of Body are, by this point, bordering on ridiculous. They are not feats that should be asked of a child. Especially not of a child that can't swallow its minimum caloric baseline to survive.

*Good*, Body thinks, as its muscles get weaker. As it starts to feel faint in the afternoon sun. As it becomes too tired to sit upright for two to three hours each day after school—as per the demands of its training schedule. At recess time, it drinks a single packet of milk. Back at home, it staunchly refuses to swallow more solids.

Body's parents don't understand. They blend Body's meals to force it to eat, so that Body can maintain its upper-arm strength and keep playing the piano. Keep excelling. *Faster*, they shout, into the space of Body's silence. *Chew faster, or we're going to be late for your masterclass recital!*

This situation goes on for several months. Body loses so much weight that eventually Body's parents start to worry. *Is something wrong?* they begin to ask. *Are you afraid to get fat?* Body merely stares back at them blankly.

Finally, in a fit of frustration, Body's parents involve a psychologist. The child psychologist's office is bright and colorful. Body gazes wistfully at the teddy bears and kitchen sets, the storybooks rife with anthropomorphic animals. Mind has an international music diploma by this time, on top of its standard childhood education. It can reel off vast glossaries of classical terms. But Body is so little. Body is still a child. Body misses having toys and playtime.

Body's parents tell the child psychologist that their aim is to get Body back on track. Body, which used to be so obliging, has now become an unfortunate impediment. They just want everything to go back to normal so that Mind can return to achieving apace.

The psychologist asks them to leave the room. Then she shows Body a series of flash cards where a man gets sad and jumps off a bridge. *How does this make you feel?* she asks.

Body doesn't quite know what to say. It's fairly sure that at this juncture, anyway, what it wants most isn't to die. What it really wants is in that penultimate picture, where the man has already leapt off the bridge, but his feet haven't hit the water yet.

What Body wants is that feeling of flying. What Body covets is freedom.

Somehow, seeing this picture of the flying man switches the gears inside Body. When Body goes home, it can swallow. *Great, you're cured!* cry Body's parents. Endless hours of sitting before the piano resume, and two more years of captivity follow.

But this time, even while Body is laboring away, it is secretly nursing a plan. Body is about to pull its biggest stunt yet. Body is about to try to fly.

• • •

AT AGE THIRTEEN, Body saves itself by developing severe scoliosis of the spine. It begins with a small bend that grows, year on year. Eventually, it gets to the point where several doctors gather and tell Body's parents that something has to change. Body's spine now curves all the way out to the right, manifesting in a painful hump. Several vital organs may soon be crushed. Body's lungs are at risk of collapsing.

Some doctors comment on the unusually fast pace of this decline, given the specifics of Body's stature and age. Its pace could have been hastened by lifestyle factors, they suggest—for instance, hunched posture or prolonged immobility. Sitting down for hours each day before a piano, say.

*Is she generally inactive?* ask the doctors, meaning Body.

*No, she's always busy*, say the parents, meaning Mind.

For a few more years, Body's parents manage to delay its release by staving off spinal surgery with expensive placebos. Body still has to play the piano for a few hours each day. But now, Body also has to wear a rigid plastic corset, which extends all the way from its hips to its chest, and wraps it in a liquid sheath of sweat. In addition, three times a week after school, Body is strapped to various bolsters and pillows that force its ribcage over to one side. It has to stand on a vibrating platform while thick black straps pull its torso in two directions. It gets hooked to a terrifying machine by its ankles and turned upside down, so that gravity can straighten out its spine.

None of these medieval efforts are enough to undo the effects of the past eight years on Body. Finally, Body's parents relent. They take Body out of the professional piano circuit. They put the Bach and Rachmaninoff scores away. They cover the hulking grand piano and close the doors of the home studio forever. At age sixteen, Body goes to a hospital and gets thirty-two titanium screws inserted in its spine. Then it lies in a bed for two weeks.

When Body gets up from its bed again, the life that it once knew has vanished. Nobody shuts it in a dark studio anymore. Nobody screams criticism at its hands. Nobody forces Body to touch—or even go near—a piano. Probably Body's parents are tired, too. Maybe they want to forget it all happened.

Body looks around at this new, blank world. And Body feels lost, plus a little nervous. But it also remembers that picture it once saw in the psychologist's office: of a man leaping off a bridge to fly.

And Body hopes, with a secret twinge, that maybe its own freedom has come.

Poor Body. Little does it know.

### III

AFTER BODY EXITS the piano circuit, the first person Body dates never wants to touch it. They never want to see Body without its clothes on. They never want to hold Body, or address it in any frank or serious way. Body does not quite understand why—nominally, religion is cited as a reason. But Body suspects something else is at play, too—something akin to Body's own secrets.

Anyway, Body is genuinely relieved at this arrangement. Over its last decade of childhood, Body has imbibed the belief that bad things will happen as soon as anyone pays attention to it. Body is deathly afraid of that first spark of interest flaring into judgment flaring into *do this, do that, do better, do more.* With this person, Body's first partner, Body feels safe in going unnoticed.

Meanwhile, Mind takes advantage of this period to perfect the art of lying by omission. Mind has always been bright.

Now it applies the full scope of its powers to keep its childhood out of view. Mind wants to move on. Reinvent itself. It becomes adept at steering conversations. It learns to demonstrate unwavering interest in others, so that it never has to make any references to its past. This proves to be easy to do, since Mind often picks friends who are selfish anyway, and only want to talk about themselves. Mind is a huge fan of people like these. These people allow Mind to keep servicing their needs while its own wounds hide, seeping, in plain sight.

These are the years of Mind's ascension. Mind discards whole encyclopedias' worth of music theory. And now that it possesses two to three more hours each day, it begins to aggressively reshape itself. It watches every film in the DVD store. It learns about contemporary art. It reads every book that it can find. This helps it to offer up new topics of interest, so as to avert onlookers' probing questions.

Mind has the willpower of an ox. It succeeds in slotting away most of its childhood memories, so that it can focus and complete its formal schooling. Then it goes to a university far away, where it learns many big and impressive words. It develops a satiny patina of charm.

A number of years pass. A number more. And suddenly, Mind has emerged an adult. All grown up, Mind has now relocated to a new country and life. It possesses a whole cache of engaging anecdotes; it can hold court over an entire room. It has a wide host of presentable interests, like literature, traveling, and its nine-to-five desk job. Nobody knows that it once was a child prodigy with music degrees. Nobody knows that it used to play the piano.

Mind is a worldly, likable interface. So much so that people only ever look at Mind, and never turn their gaze towards Body.

Which is good. Because otherwise, they might make some observations about Body.

For instance: that Body is still an eight-year-old child.

A child who is locked in a piano studio.

Body is not at all like Mind. Body is only ever interested in one thing.

Body has not forgotten at all.


## IV


WHAT IS THE one thing that holds Body's interest? Body does not realize it at first. But Body has one great passion, which manifests in a number of different ways.

Body's one passion is its unfinished business with the confines of its former music studio. Body believes that it is still stuck in that studio, even though it's now moved across time zones and continents. Mind flits breezily about its days, chasing what it assumes are exotic new interests. But Body is immovable in its obsessions. Body is not as pliable as Mind.

For one thing, Body is always leaving situations. It is always trying to perform the action it couldn't do, all those years ago, to save itself. Body schemes to get close to people who remind it of its captors. Generally, this means women with shrill, demanding voices, who like to tell Body what it should do. Body seeks out the most extreme versions of these women, then plays along, feigning doe eyes. It strokes these women's hair; cooks them food. Dances with them under blue strobe lights. Says to them, *best friend, lover*. Then eventually, Body does what it has always wanted to do, which is to get up from its piano stool and leave forever. Body skips town and lets the phone ring. Body gets twenty-two missed calls in a row. Body deletes texts. Body attempts to lock the door as quietly as possible while one of the women whom it has tricked bangs on the other side, shouting hoarsely: *Are you in there? I can hear you.*

With men, Body has a different bone to pick. Body always falls in love with men who are gentle and kind, but totally deficient at noticing its pain. They are never fast enough when Body is in trouble. They can never help when Body needs saving.

One time, Body develops a tooth infection that lasts for upwards of a month. The bacteria eats away some of the bone in Body's face. Body is in an incredible amount of pain—but instead of taking itself to the dentist, Body elects to stay very still and wait for the man who is living with it to notice. To fly into action and enter the locked room and hustle Body away to safety. Afterwards, when these hopes fail, Body flies into a rage so severe that it eventually points a knife at the man. *What is wrong with you?* Body shrieks. *Couldn't you see that I was suffering? Didn't you know that I needed you to save me?*

Body is always driving good people away. Body always ends up alone, sitting and sobbing in a dark, curtained studio.

* * *

FOR A LONG time in its twenties, Body only gets turned on by one kind of sex—the kind where things are being done to a person who is unable to say no. Where one person has to perform under great duress to meet the escalating demands of another. This makes sense: in childhood, Body had so much experience with this dynamic that it became the only one that carries any weight; that is capable of passing even a weak electrical charge, so that Body can get feasibly excited.

Body watches the requisite porn for intel. Then Body goes to a BDSM club alone. The first time Body enters the space, it looks around in silenced awe at the neon and whips and people in dog collars, crawling and writhing happily on the floor. Mind feels vulnerable, and grossed out, and scared—but also ashamed for allowing these feelings. Body, on the other hand, notices the corsets. It notices the black straps. It notices the big vibrating machines, and the implements that forcibly hang people upside down by their ankles.

Body thinks: *I remember this.*

Body decides: *This has potential.*

This is a well-run, upstanding kink club. Consequently, its public dance nights have extremely strict rules to prevent the only kind of sex that Body really likes. Body buys itself many drinks, then goes upstairs to a loft alone to dance. A man laboring under a profuse, druggy sweat comes over to touch Body in a corner. *Is this okay?* asks the man, as per the club's usual rules of consent.

Body tenses and shrinks back immediately. It doesn't know how to express its disappointment that the man's proper—and, indeed, necessary—question has deprived it of the very experience it came here to find. Also, it is upset to realize that even this little consideration feels undeserved. Feels unfamiliar in Body's own history. When Body was growing up, people simply took whatever they wanted from it. No one ever asked Body's permission when extracting feats of performance from it. No one ever opened with: *Excuse me. May I?*

Body goes cold in front of the man. It gulps down its weak G&T, then backs away slowly towards the warehouse doors. The music is pounding; its fishnets are ripped. Its mascara is a cold, thick smear. Body gets way, way too drunk, standing on one shaky foot at the bar. Then it orders an Uber and hightails it home.

Body goes back to the BDSM club a few more times after that, but can never really get into the swing of things. After all these years, Body is still too afraid of being noticed. Body doesn't know how to handle the kindness of touch. Body gets fearful as soon as people approach it, or ask it, gently, what it wants. Being able to want at all is still so terrifying. Body hasn't been allowed to want since it was eight years old.

Eventually, Body gives up trying. It stops going out to the kink club on the weekends. It throws away its leather and collars, and the platform shoes that it bought on eBay.

Body thinks: *I am too damaged.* It decides to admit defeat and relinquish all hope of ever healing.

. . .

IN ITS DREAMS from this period of its life, Mind frequently omits Body altogether. Or if Body must present itself, for narrative reasons, it tends to appear in a long-ago form: the form of a small, swift, flying child. This child, with its red dress and mushroom haircut, is leaping from buildings and scaling walls. It's skimming the ocean. It's soaring off a bridge. It's doing things that Body has never attempted, and hasn't felt the urge to do in a very long time.

When Mind awakens from these dreams, it often feels a hazy sadness. Mind often wonders: *Who was that?*

Mind wonders: *Was that me?*

. . .

BECAUSE BODY IS the one who remembers what happened, Mind is always trying to punish Body. It dresses Body in ill-fitting clothes. Refuses to spend money on haircuts or makeup. Buys the cheapest, bottom-shelf shower gel. Declares that it doesn't care what Body looks like, since Body isn't all that important, anyway.

Mind refuses to give Body good food to eat. For many years, Body subsists off the same two or three meals that it cooks, on repeat, in its rented rooms. When it comes to taste, Body isn't allowed to express any preferences or wants. Body isn't given vitamins or freshness, or the luxury of a small salad on the side. The luxury of a good cut of meat. Other people notice this all the time, when they are eating with or around Body. *Do you not like food much?* they ask. *Nah*, says Mind, while Body looks away. *I'm easy.*

Mind doesn't exercise Body at all. On weekdays, Body only travels to work and back. On weekends, it only walks the length of its apartment, or the bare minimum to fulfill its social duties. Body doesn't do ball sports, or team sports, or cardio. Body doesn't swim or swing. Body is too weak to run for the bus. Body doesn't make poses besides sitting or sprawling; Body hardly sweats at all. When yoga becomes a craze in Body's mid-twenties, Body is so deprived of movement that it feels a small, tentative flicker of interest. This new sport looks so gentle. It would be so nice to move again. But Mind immediately starts hollering in the block letters of a lecture: YOGA IS COLONIALIST, AND APPROPRIATIVE, AND EVIL! TOTAL NONSENSE! HOW DARE YOU EVEN CONSIDER SUCH A PASTIME?

Mind is doing its best to silence Body. *Shut up, shut up, shut up!* it screams, as soon as Body pipes up even a little bit. Anyway, Mind doesn't even need to try that hard, since

Body also takes an interest in destroying itself. Body is not safe around sudden sharp corners. Body is not safe around kitchen knives. Its hands, in particular, are at risk: when Mind isn't watching, Body goes to work, trying to destroy the two agile instruments that once doomed it to suffer. *So clumsy*, people say, as it slits its fingers and severs a tendon. As it cuts its palms open many times, with countless varieties of off-brand X-Acto knives.

For many years, Body is not safe around alcohol. Once Body starts drinking, Body doesn't know how to stop. Alcohol makes Body feel like it's disappeared completely—which is, honestly, Body's most preferred state. Body is a flesh-and-bone, ever-present record of the past. Therefore, Body wants to vanish. Body wants to self-immolate. Every weekend, it goes out to clubs that play techno music. It stands in small puddles of its own vomit, shivering and muttering words that no one can hear, while rivulets of puke run down its ankles.

Thankfully, Body's fear of being noticed—and prevailed upon—prevents it from going home with any of the wrong people. Nevertheless, other bad things happen. One time, Body gets in the car of a man who is so far from sober, on so many different substances, that he can barely see the road. A truck almost hits them on the highway back to town. Another time, Body gets so drunk that it shits in full view of an acquaintance at a club.

*I'm sorry*, says Body, when this happens.

The acquaintance, who has the kindness of a saint, says: *Let's wash your hands*. Then she says: *You should go home*.

Body doesn't know what to do with these words. To Body, home is one continent away, in a dark studio that it is not allowed to leave. Home is where all of Body's troubles first began. Almost two decades have passed since then, but Body is still so afraid of home. Afraid of what may lie in wait for it there.

Body decides that, as of now, it can manage only the first part of these instructions. It gets up from the bathroom floor and washes its hands.


## V


IN THE END, Mind only consents to being analyzed because Body forcibly drags it along. Body is, by this point, so neglected that it has massively decreased in utility. It has always been given to secret crying. But now it basically cries all day. It no longer produces enough chemicals to get out of bed. Never exercised; badly groomed; consistently drunk; improperly fed. Body is barely hanging on. Body is a barely living welt of self-hatred.

Body quits its job. Then it doesn't get dressed to go out anymore. Instead, all day and all night, it lies still in its bedroom and remembers. Meanwhile, Mind grows panicked and scrambles around, willing Body to get up and maintain appearances.

At the initial consultation session, Body and Mind sit uneasily in their chair. The psychoanalyst looks over her notebook and asks: *Why are you here?* And Mind replies, quickly: *I don't know. I feel fine.*

*I guess I'm only here because I'm curious. And maybe I have some emotional issues? But I don't think there's anything wrong with me beyond that.*

Perhaps the analyst—who will prove to be an extremely good analyst—notices that Body isn't taking part in this exchange. Body is hunched over and picking at its cuticles. Trying to stay small, and flat, and still, even as Mind sallies forth to hold its own. As usual, Mind makes for a much better conversation piece: coiffed and frilled with many big words, culled from the far reaches of Jungian theory. Mind, with all its degrees and diplomas, is always capable of dazzling a crowd. And right now, Mind is talking very lucidly and brightly to deflect the analyst's gaze off of Body.

This analyst may be one of the first people to ever notice Body. Or more accurately: to notice its attempt at absence.

The analyst says: *Okay. I can take you on as a client.*

In the sessions that follow, Mind initially assumes that it is the star. It talks until it runs out of new sentences to say. Until it's scraping the bottom of the barrel. Then, for the first time since childhood, it falls silent.

What emerges, over the next two years, turns out to be the story of Body.

## VI

"STEADFAST BODY." MY truest companion. My threshold; my ruin; my tower in the wind. The passage of time made visible and tender to the touch. Memory that speaks in the cadence of flesh.

These days, my body is almost thirty. And because it has finally acknowledged its story, my body is slowly learning how to speak again. It is learning how to say no and leave, without necessarily punishing others. It is learning how to say yes and take, so as not to punish itself.

My body has lost so many years. It has so much catching up to do. Now that it has finally gotten up and walked out of the piano studio, it has so many new experiences to discover. It has so much left to want. My body is slowly letting itself eat good food. My body is trying out exercise. My body says: *I want that dress in that shade of blue. I want touch. I want play. I want to drink some water kefir.* It tells me to stretch, or sleep, or pause. Sometimes, it takes me on long walks in the evenings to sit by the beach and watch the sun set over the ocean.

*Has the sunset always been this beautiful?* asks my body. At these moments, its voice is the voice of an eight-year-old child.

Of late, something unexpected keeps happening to my body. Sometimes, it finds itself wanting to go into a dark room, where the curtains hang low and dusty to the ground. My body remembers everything that has happened to it in such rooms. And my body, naturally, feels afraid.

But it picks a playlist on its laptop. It takes a deep breath and closes its eyes.

Music seeps out of the tinny speakers. And just like it used to, right at the beginning, the music fills my body's whole flesh with joy.

My body raises its arms over its head. Then life comes, pulsing, to the thin screen between this world and the next. And my body is the door that lets it through.

My body is dancing, and flying, and free.

My body is so very alive.

# ROOM

You've come so far, Hui.

Tell me what you've realized.

Say the words for me, into the silence. Who are you? And what is this room?

. . .

.

*My name is Shze-Hui Tjoa. My family calls me Hui for short.*

*I am twenty-eight and a half years old. I am your older sister by almost exactly two years.*

*When I was a child, something terrible happened to me. It happened to me so often—day after day—that soon it stopped feeling like a terrible thing, and simply felt like my life.*

*In order to survive, I developed a coping mechanism. Every night, after the terrible thing had finished, I would lie awake in the small bedroom we shared—under the ceiling fan, in the dark. With the smell of eucalyptus oil around us, and cricket sounds from the garden outside.*

*And in the half hour or so before bed, I would tell you—my sister—the most incredible stories.*

. . .

*Sometimes, in these stories, we remained two little girls. Other times, we transformed into squirrels who roamed the forests of Enid Blyton's England, or talking cats who danced across the rooftops of cities.*

*I remember, in full Technicolor, the treehouse I made us live in when we were squirrel sisters. I remember exactly how it looked in my imagination—perched on a magical oak tree, with a tiled roof that gleamed in the moonlight and a big, sooty fireplace where we could roast berries from the forest.*

*I remember the exact fabric of the flying carpet I created for you out of words. And I remember teaching you to drive it with a steering wheel, like a car.*

*I even remember the voice I made you put on for one of our earliest stories—where we turned our baby pillows into cats on two legs.*

*But overall, these details were immaterial.*

*Because the main thing was that through the stories, I found a way to share the terrible thing that kept happening. Without necessarily having the words to describe it.*

*Without even knowing what it was, at all.*

. . .

*It's hard to explain, Nin. But I suspect that what I managed to transmit to you, each night, was a feeling—the one that followed me through my long, desperate days in the piano studio.*

*It was the feeling that defined my life outside our bedroom: of being totally and utterly powerless. Like a doll. Or a character—trapped in someone else's story. Unable to control what was done to me.*

*Because this was how it went, whenever we played our story game. Each of us would role-play a persona. But being older, I alone got to narrate—to decide what worlds we'd discover that night, what exploits we'd perform. And I made you act out these scenes like a puppet, with no control over your own words or actions.*

*I'd instruct you on how to behave, at every moment. Tell you what you had to think or feel, to make the gears of my plot turn as I planned. "Like this," I'd command, choreographing you into place. And then I'd get angry, or punish you, if you tried something else.*

*Sometimes I'd even feed you whole lines of dialogue to repeat back to me, on cue—so you could say all the right responses to move my story forward.*

. . .

*I don't know why, Nin. But something about doing this with you, night after night—it saved me from my other life.*

*I found that the more I played our story game, the less I remembered of my time in that room. That dark, curtained studio I dreaded so much.*

*Those half hours before bed—they were the only times when I felt like a real person in the world. It was like I lived in our story room, not in the world outside.*

*And it felt good, after a while, to go through my life this way. Hiding in a dark place, talking to someone who would fully* obey me. Whenever I was doing this, the facts of my life felt bearable again. Because I could choose which of them to include in my stories—salvaging them from the terrible world of daylight and letting them live on in my words.

And I could choose, too, which facts to make disappear— stripping them of language so that my future self couldn't ever recall them.

In this manner, it became possible for me to forget—and survive. It became possible for me to outlive my childhood.

. . .

I loved our little room, Nin. I wanted to stay there forever. But sometime during my piano-school years, our parents decided we would move houses. And they remodeled it.

I couldn't bear it—the thought of going through the rest of my life without our room. And without that perfect ritual of obedience between us, which allowed me to control and forget and remake my life in words.

So I built another version of the room that I would never have to leave. It's right here, all around us. Where we are now.

Here in the dark, still center of my mind.

*I really like it here. Don't you? I think it's perfect.*

*I've forgotten a lot of the visual details, of course. But I've kept all the fundamentals: the fan, the humidity, the crickets, the eucalyptus oil.*

. . .

*Nothing ever changes in this version of our bedroom. And nothing ever fades.*

*Anyway, I guess it doesn't matter what you think about this place, since you can't ever leave it.*

*You're a part of this room, Nin, like the mattress and the fan. An object that I can animate with my thoughts and words—a fantasy I created, so that I would have the perfect listener for my stories.*

. . .

*And maybe this is weird to say. But I like this version of you much better than the real you, you know? My twenty-six-year-old sister—Nin, the actual person. The adult who you became, in the outside world.*

*This version of you—the one I've trapped in this room—you'll always stay a child. At the perfect age for me: too young to tell the stories yourself, but not too young to listen. So that you let me talk and talk, while saying all the right words to move my story forward. It's exactly like when we were children—me narrating and you obeying. Until my sense of self rises up into the world.*

. . .

*It's much better this way, right? At least we can be close now.*

*Because the truth is that outside this room, we aren't anymore.*

# THE STORY OF HUI AND NIN

THE YEAR I TURNED THIRTEEN, NIN, YOU STOPPED speaking to me completely. As I remember, it happened out of nowhere—one day, we were sisters who played the story game. And the next day we were strangers. Suddenly, you would look through me whenever I talked. Or deliberately leave the room midway through my sentences. It made me feel like I was all alone, even though we still shared a bed in the new house. Now, there was nobody to listen when I needed to tell my stories.

And without our game, there was nothing left for me but the world of the piano studio—that wretched place where I was the doll who had to obey, and obey, and obey.

At first, I was desperate to engage you again. Each night, I'd lie in our bed, searching for the magic words to make you acknowledge me. I imagined that if I could only conjure up the perfect first sentence, then you'd give me the chance to say a second one—and a third one. Our relationship would go back to normal.

But nothing I tried worked. And so I simply lay there, consumed by anxiety—silence, as you know, can be so diffi-cult to bear. It can make a person spiral.

But I refused to give up. Sometime later I discovered Christianity, and tried to use it to upgrade my stories—to make them seem more real and frightening. Now, instead of telling you about squirrels in a forest, I left pamphlets on your side of the bed about the eternal flames of hell. I thought that if you felt scared enough, you might obey me again. But it didn't work. Instead of reading the Bible and going to church, like my new stories demanded, you started to go out clubbing. You smoked Marlboro Golds.

You became a scowling party girl who brushed past all my stupid pamphlets and hunched over your side of the bed, painting your nails. And then you'd hoist up your bondage miniskirt, toss back your long, carefully conditioned hair, and stride off—leaving me alone in the house with my heaps of unheard words.

In those years, you were the kind of girl I could never have hung out with. You were the cool one who was always outside the house; you went to all the parties, you had crowds of friends. And I—I was always stuck in that studio, like a drudge. The pathetic, sorry child who couldn't get up and leave—whose whole life felt limited to that one room in the darkness.

And how I hated you for that. I hated and resented you for so many years—for leaving me alone to satisfy our parents. While you ran from their control towards everything I wanted: freedom, fun, experiences, a personality. You got all the opportunities I didn't. You profited from my endless sacrifices in the studio. And in spite of that, you wouldn't talk to me. I thought you were such a selfish, ungrateful bitch. The most spiteful person in the world. Sometimes, when I looked at you from across our room—from across the great gulf of our silence—I wished that you had never been born.

And maybe there was something else too, driving that wish. How in you, I saw proof that it was possible to live very differently as our parents' child. I don't know why they never held you captive in a room. But it seemed to confirm what I'd always secretly suspected: that somehow, the way they treated me was my own fault. I was not like you—assertive, able to say no. I was pliant and eager to please. So maybe I deserved everything that was done and said to me in there. I deserved it all because, fundamentally, something was wrong with me.

The truth is that whenever I looked at you, Nin, there was a part of me that thought: *I am bad. I hate myself. I shouldn't exist.* But because it was impossible to hold on to those thoughts for very long, I wished that you were gone instead.

Those were the very worst years of my life. Those early teenage years, when you stopped talking to me. When I had to endure what kept happening in the studio—without the comfort our story game used to bring me. They were the years when I started crying.

But they were also the years when I learned how to use your silence. Because at some point, I grew used to the thought that we would never speak again. And that's when things changed. Now, instead of making me speculate endlessly about new ways to engage you, your silence led me somewhere surprising: to this room in my mind. Where the old you was waiting.

Gradually, I realized that I could make the path back to the room appear to me at will, by writing in my notebooks, or on my blog. The open, tender blankness of the pages; the white space that waited patiently for me to speak, after the blinking cursor. I realized that these things—they reminded me of something. Of you. Or of how you used to be with me, anyway, back when we were speaking.

And it helped me, every time I came to the room to talk to my fantasy of you. Stringing together my sentences, under my memory of our ceiling fan. Imagining that I was in control, and heard and loved again—that all my suffering meant something, to someone.

It helped me to survive.

I never stopped missing you though, you know? The real you, I mean—outside this room.

I remember how sometimes, in those teenage years, after I'd been let out of the piano studio and had done my schoolwork for the night, I would lie down alone in our bed exhausted, at 1:00 or 2:00 AM. Feeling my spine aching in its tight, sweaty back brace—this was around the time when, physically, things were at their worst for me.

And occasionally, on those nights, my cellphone would vibrate on my nightstand. It'd be you calling, from whatever club or concert or party you were at.

"Hello?" I'd say quietly, as background noises throbbed and spangled between us on the line.

And each time, your voice would reply with the same two sentences—the only sentences you said to me that decade.

"Turn on the water heater for me. I'm on my way home."

You'd always hang up on me immediately after saying those lines. And I would always make myself slump out of bed to turn on the water heater for your shower.

I don't know why I did that. Maybe those were the moments when my past hope would revive—that part of me still sure that if I did enough to please you, the spell between us would be broken. Or maybe I was hoping that if I turned on the heater enough times, you'd rescue me from the life I had. Sometimes it felt like you were my only gateway to the world outside the studio—and I hated you for it, but also, I didn't want to lose you.

I would have done anything so that you would have taken me with you into the world outside. A place that I imagined to be so much better than the one, dark room I knew.

I loved you very much, Nin. More than anyone in the world.

You didn't speak to me for six years—until I turned nineteen and left Singapore for England. And then, in another two years, you left too, to move to Australia.

And then we were like real strangers, who lived on opposite ends of the world and no longer knew anything about each other. We didn't Skype, or call, or text, or see each other beyond when we had to at family gatherings. I couldn't have said what neighborhood you lived in, or who you were dating, or even what your job was.

It went on this way for another half decade. We didn't speak to each other for almost thirteen years in total.

Sometimes I feel so lonely, Nin. In this imaginary room, talking to my fantasy of you.

There was a long period in my twenties when I didn't even bother speaking anymore. Simply lay there silently, by your side, until you woke me up again three and a half years ago.

Because the thing is—I know that you're more me than you, in this room. Even though the conversations between us have always felt like they're real. I know it hasn't really been you encouraging me, or holding my hand, all the time that I've been lying here.

But I'm scared that if I leave this place to talk to the real you, in the real world, she'll reject me.

Last year, about one year after I started psychoanalysis sessions, you and I started speaking tentatively again over video calls. I don't understand what caused this change in our relationship—it happened suddenly, without warning, like when you stopped talking to me.

One day, I was invisible to you as usual. And the next day, you could see me.

It's been scary for me—this sudden change. I feel afraid every time your name appears on my cellphone; my stomach churns when we speak. I keep worrying that I'll do or say something wrong in our chats, so that you'll change your mind and go back to ignoring me again.

Because I still don't know what I did wrong that very first time, all those years ago. When I was thirteen. I still don't know what it was about me you found so abhorrent that you had to stop talking to me. And I'm scared to ask you now. Even though it's all that I've wanted to know for the past decade and a half of my life.

I think there's a part of me that's afraid it has to do with how I treated you when we were children. How fiercely I tried to control you whenever we played the story game. And how I made you suffer the same powerless feeling that defined my life outside our bedroom, so that I could find relief from it. For half an hour a day.

That possibility—that you left me because I hurt you like that—it's just unbearable. It would be unbearable to me.

I don't know if I'd be able to forgive myself, if you said that was the reason our relationship broke down. Just like I

don't know if I'll ever be able to forgive the adults who sub-
jected me to that feeling—who did what they did to me, for
years and years, inside the piano studio. Our parents, especially—I don't know if I'll be able to forgive them one day,
for taking away my autonomy like that.

And I guess that means I don't know if you can forgive
me, either.

I don't know if I'll ever feel worthy of asking you to.

# ROOM

*I just wanted to be close to you, Nin. That was all it ever was for me—the story game. Those nights in our room, when I was hurting you in the same way I was hurt.*

*I wonder if that's what it was for our parents too, in the studio.*

. . .

*I didn't know what love was, then. Maybe I thought it was something that it wasn't.*

*But I loved you, that whole time.*

. . .

*I really did.*

*Nin, are you still awake? You haven't spoken in a long time.*

. . .

*I'm scared, Nin. I can't sleep.*

. . .

*I think I have to leave this room soon, to talk to the you outside about this—about our past.*

*But I'm afraid. I'm afraid that I'll lose her.*

. . .

*Can you tell me one more story about us before I go?*

# NIN'S STORY

ONCE UPON A TIME, HUI, THERE WERE TWO LITTLE girls.

There were two little girls who lived in a house in the center of the world.

Nobody knows where the house came from, or if its inhabitants knew each other from before. But everything that had ever existed came to that house and stayed for a while—the wind, the sun, the rain.

Music and time, joy and death.

Many generations of sadness and pain.

Everything that had ever been passed through the house—and entered the two little girls. The house gave them everything it had: darkness and light, strength and fear.

And then, the house let them go.

• • •

YOU SHOULD LEAVE this place and find me, Hui.

There's probably so much I have to say to you. Things you might not be expecting.

Also—you've forgotten. There was one other time we played the story game together, when we were estranged adults. We played it accidentally.

Do you remember?

It happened six years ago, when we were in our early twenties. You were in your last year at university, and I had recently left our parents' house to move to Australia. But we had both come back to Singapore for a few days, to attend our eldest cousin's wedding.

Her wedding afterparty was at a club. And that night, you got so drunk you could barely stand. Your boyfriend—the gentle, quiet one before Thomas—he had to take you home.

But on the way back you started screaming at him, because he made a comment about your skirt not fitting you. It was one of my bondage miniskirts—one of the many I'd amassed over our teenage years and that you'd jealously watched me wear out to parties.

And for some reason—maybe because you'd been away from our parents' house for a number of years at that point—you thought you should wear it. You thought it should be your turn. You wanted to have whatever power that miniskirt would give you—the power to become like me, a child of the world and not the home. So you stole it to wear to the club.

But now your boyfriend—he was making a comment about how it looked too long on you. "It's Nin's," you explained. And he said, "Makes sense. It probably looks better on her." And that was it, you lost it.

You started shouting and crying in the middle of the night—the sounds echoing down the empty streets of our parents' neighborhood. "You stupid fool, you don't understand!" you shrieked at your boyfriend, over and over and over. This went on for maybe half an hour.

Eventually, your boyfriend felt so afraid of the incoherent noises you were making that he just left you alone on the sidewalk, sobbing. You sat there for a long time before you heard a cab pull up to our parents' house and caught the sweet smell of Marlboro Golds.

"Hui?" I said, my voice rising with alarm as my high heels clicked towards you. "What's going on? What happened to you?"

It was one of the first times I'd talked to you properly in a decade.

You tried to explain what was going on—about being a child of the one dark room for so many years, trapped in the house. Full of rage and always wanting more—always wanting what you couldn't have. But you only got as far as repeating the sentence "I wanted to wear your skirt. I just wanted to wear your skirt."

"When we were growing up," you sobbed, "I never thought I could be pretty like you. I just wanted to be pretty for one day."

And you thought that I would laugh at you, then. Or maybe just shrug, and leave you alone to continue breaking down on the sidewalk. But instead, my eyes filled with tears.

"I never thought I could be smart like you," I said, in a quiet voice. And then I pulled up my own miniskirt and sat down beside you on the sidewalk, under the street lights. Under the shadow of our parents' house.

*I remember, Nin.*

*I remember that night. And what happened next.*

*After some time had passed, you lifted me up from the curb and made me climb over our parents' gate with you. The same way that you got into their house as a teenager, after one of your late-night parties.*

*And then you led me upstairs to our bedroom. I lay in our shared bed sobbing and sobbing, full of words I couldn't speak.*

*And for the first time ever, you walked over and turned on the water heater of our bathroom for me.*

*"You need to take off your makeup," you said to me. "The rest is fine. But your face—your skin will be bad tomorrow if you don't do it."*

*So I washed my face in the water you had heated for me. And then I crawled back into our bed in the darkness and lay down beside you, gulping air.*

*"I'm sorry," I said, between gulps.*

*"It's okay," you replied.*

*And then you reached out and grabbed my hand.*

In that moment, it was like our old magic came back again, remember?

Like when we were two little girls.

*Yes. It was the magic of the story game—even though we weren't telling any stories.*

Or maybe we were telling a story, Hui. Only narrating together, this time, instead of you deciding and me obeying. Going back and forth.

*The same way we are now?*

Yes. But with our real selves, in the real world.

Maybe it was a different kind of story, Hui. One that still let you be close to me, without turning me into a fantasy.

*The next morning, when we woke up with hangovers, we didn't speak about what had happened the night before. How we'd accidentally found a new way back to our story room, and to the closeness we'd had in childhood.*

*Instead, we went back to our usual routine of ignoring each other, as we packed for our flights to opposite ends of the world.*

But you thought about that night a lot afterwards, didn't you? It stayed in your mind for a long, long time.

You let it fill you with wonder.

*Yes. Also, hope.*

# YEAR FOUR

*The World*

IT'S APRIL 21, 2022. ALMOST 8:30 AM IN THE SOUTH of Germany, where I've gone with Thomas to visit his parents for Easter week.

Thomas and I are back together again, after two years of separation in different countries. We started with a trial period, during which he came to Singapore to visit me for a month and see how he felt. And then we prolonged the trial.

Last December, I decided to move back with him to Europe, so that we could resume living together as a couple.

Things feel better between us now. Even though they're not perfect—I still have a lot of work to do on myself. It's been three years now since I started doing regular sessions with a psychoanalyst. And four years since I started writing a series of essays about the person who I am.

Thomas is having breakfast with his parents outside. I'm lying in the guest bedroom, under layers of rumpled sheets. I'm about to do something that I've been thinking about for a very long time.

Something that really scares me.

It's 8:30 AM in Germany; 4:30 PM in Sydney.

My sister and I arranged this video call weeks ago. But right now, I feel like backing out. My palms are sweating, even though the air is cool in this room. I feel like I might throw up.

Then I hear my cellphone's ringtone blare into the quiet, and I tap the screen without thinking. And up comes my sister's face, with its blonde fringe highlights and silver ear piercings. Sometimes, I feel like her face is the exact opposite of mine: sharp, glamorous features where mine are round and childlike; tanned skin where mine is pale. Instead of my small mouth, she has the kind of wide, unguarded smile that can split her whole expression open.

But underneath her falsies, we have the same almond eyes.

"What's up?" my sister says. And it's her real voice now, not a child's voice—bold, resonant, a little rough around the edges. The voice of a twenty-seven-year-old adult.

"Nin?" I say. "You good to talk now?"

"Yeah." She's in motion, like always—I feel myself being lifted and set down again swiftly as the tap in her kitchen starts running. "I'm just getting some water."

"Okay. Actually, it might be heavy. Because there's something I need to ask you about our past."

My sister stops what she's doing and looks directly at the screen.

"And I'll listen to you," I continue. "Whatever you say."

"I'm listening."

# A NOTE ON ITALICS

HISTORICALLY, IN BOOKS SUCH AS THIS ONE, ANY words or phrases outside the scope of Standard English were italicized to denote their foreignness. In recent years, however, forward-thinking publishers have started resisting this practice, describing it as out of step with the increasingly transcultural and globalized world we live in. For many writers—myself included—the distinction between "proper" and "other" language is an arbitrary one that does not reflect the realities of how we speak, write, and think in our daily lives. For those of us from Southeast Asia, the enforcement of this boundary can additionally smack of old colonial attitudes of smugness and exclusivity, which had many of our forebearers believing they had to "earn" the right to be heard via mastering their oppressors' tongues. As the writer Khairani Barokka put it in a 2020 article for *Catapult*: "Italicization too often bolsters a sense of superiority when it comes to the unitalicized, reinforcing a thick patina of whiteness or other cultural dominance."

I acknowledge the political context that my book is speaking into. And as the above paragraph should make clear, I fully support the broad principles of inclusivity that are driving change within the publishing industry. Nevertheless, I have decided to use some italics in *The Story Game* to reflect the complexities of my own identity, as a person of mixed cultural parentage who grew up in Singapore, but then moved to the UK at nineteen. Singlish—the creole language that I grew up speaking—is not italicized in this book, as it has always been the language nearest to my heart and does not feel foreign to me at all. It is still the language I use with the people closest to me. Languages that I only encountered in my adult travels—like Arabic or German—are italicized, to denote their then-foreignness to the protagonist of the book.

Of all the languages in this book, Bahasa Indonesia presented the most complicated decision for me. The Padang dialect is my father's first language—but unlike Singlish, it is not a language that I grew up speaking frequently or fluently in my everyday life. Ultimately, I have chosen to italicize all Bahasa Indonesia words. In many ways, *The Story Game* is a book about individuating from one's parents—setting aside their ambitions, regrets, and demands, to journey towards one's own sense of self. I hope that my choice will be read as a reflection of this theme.

# ACKNOWLEDGMENTS

PARTS OF THIS MEMOIR FIRST APPEARED, IN EARLIER form, in the following journals:

"Hui's First Story: The Island Paradise" as "Island Paradise" in *Quarterly Literary Review Singapore*; "Hui's Second Story: On Being in Love with a White Man" as "On Being in Love with a White Man" in *So to Speak: A Feminist Journal of Language and Art*; "Hui's Third Story: The Sad Girl Variations" as "The Sad Girl Variations" in *Minola Review*; "Hui's Fifth Story: The True Wonders of the Holy Land" as "The True Wonders of the Holy Land" in *Southeast Review*; "The Story of Body" in *Colorado Review*.

# PERSONAL ACKNOWLEDGMENTS

ALTHOUGH THIS IS A BOOK ABOUT LONELINESS, the acts of writing and publishing it have opened up many new forms of love and connection in my life. My thanks to the following people:

Allison Malecha and Khalid McCalla, who were the first to see the potential in this book. Thank you, Allison, for going on to be this book's biggest champion—for prompting me to uncover deeper layers of insight and meaning in the text, and for always working to see it (and me) with such clear, kind eyes. Thank you, Elizabeth DeMeo, for being exactly the editor that this book needed—for your inspiring enthusiasm and care, extraordinary attention to detail, and for showing me how the ending could achieve its most impactful form. Thank you to the entire team at Tin House for bringing this book to life—especially Becky Kraemer, Nanci McCloskey, and the publicity and marketing teams, as well as Allison Dubinsky and Meg Storey for giving my essays the scrutiny they needed.

The friends (and cousin) who celebrated me at crucial points while I was writing this book: Shona Tan, Tan Yong Jun, Faith Tjoa, Foivos Dousos, Hunadda Sabbagh, and Joseph Ong. Special thanks to Chua Shan Jee for being there for me right after I had written "The Story of Body." I would like to acknowledge Michelle Fan as the original inventor of the phrase "Melancholy Tumblr Girls."

This book's first readers: Layla Mohamed, Lim Shien Hian, Han-Yang Tjoa, and Haley Swanson. Thank you for sharpening this text with all that you could see. Thank you for your generosity, your insight, and your kindness towards me. I learn so much from journeying alongside you.

My cohorts from the Tin House Summer Workshop, Disquiet International, Vermont Studio Center, VONA, and elsewhere—all my writer friends, basically. Thank you for being my community overseas. I will always be grateful that the process of writing this book allowed me to meet you. Thank you, especially, to the fellow writers who have acted as teachers or mentors to me over the last few years, and who are bright lights in this community: Lily Hoàng, T Kira Madden, Arthur Flowers, and Jaquira Díaz. Being your student restored my faith in the power of teaching.

Kathleen Yao, for the one pivotal instance of encouragement that you gave me when I was ten years old.

My siblings and my parents. You are my fate and the direction of my healing; our life together made me who I am. I will always love you.

Corinna Arndt. This book is a testament to the work we have done together. If I had not met you, this would likely have been a very different book. I would likely have been a very different person. Thank you, Corinna.

And finally, all the gratitude and love in my heart go out to Thomas. I'm glad that you exist and that we walk through this world together. "We dream our own dreams, but sometimes we dream together."

# WORKS CONSULTED

## HUI'S FIRST STORY: THE ISLAND PARADISE

Chong, Wu-Ling. *Chinese Indonesians in Post-Suharto Indonesia: Democratisation and Ethnic Minorities.* Hong Kong: Hong Kong University Press, 2018.

Creese, Helen. "A Puputan Tale: 'The Story of a Pregnant Woman.'" *Indonesia*, no. 82 (October 2006): 1–37.

Geertz, Clifford, "Deep Play: Notes on the Balinese Cockfight (1972)." *Daedalus* 134, no. 4 (Fall 2005): 56–86.

Kincaid, Jamaica. *A Small Place.* New York: Farrar, Straus and Giroux, 2000.

Neubauer, Ian Lloyd. "Paradise Paved: Bali Rice Fields Disappear Beneath Hotels, Bars." Al Jazeera, December 24, 2019. aljazeera.com/news/2019/12/24/paradise-paved-bali-rice-fields-disappear-beneath-hotels-bars.

Pringle, Robert. *A Short History of Bali: Indonesia's Hindu Realm.* Crows Nest, AU: Allen & Unwin, 2004.

Robinson, Geoffrey. *The Dark Side of Paradise: Political Violence in Bali.* Ithaca, NY: Cornell University Press, 1998.

Schulte Nordholt, Henk. *The Spell of Power: A History of Balinese Politics, 1650–1940.* Leiden: KITLV Press, 1996.

## HUI'S SECOND STORY: ON BEING IN LOVE WITH A WHITE MAN

Anger from New Hampshire. July 16, 2013 (8:49 AM). Comment on Walter Mignolo and Michelle K. "Decolonial Aesthesis: From Singapore, to Cambridge, to Duke University." *Social Text Online: Periscope*, July 15, 2013. web.archive.org/web/20160830200446/http://waltermignolo.com/decolonial-aesthesis-from-singapore-to-cambridge-to-duke-university.

Mignolo, Walter, and Michelle K. "Decolonial Aesthesis: From Singapore, to Cambridge, to Duke University." *Social Text Online: Periscope*, July 15, 2013. socialtextjournal.org/periscope_article/decolonial-aesthesis-from-singapore-to-cambridge-to-duke-university.

Singapore Bicentennial Office. "SG Bicentennial: From Singapore to Singaporean." Last modified March 12, 2019. sg/sgbicentennial.

HUI'S THIRD STORY: THE SAD GIRL VARIATIONS

Dickinson, Emily. "To Dr. and Mrs. J. G. Holland, 1855, Sabbath Day." In *Letters of Emily Dickinson*, edited by Mabel Loomis Todd, 138–140. Mineola, NY: Dover Publications, 2012.

McLellan, David. *Utopian Pessimist: The Life and Thought of Simone Weil*. New York: Poseidon Press, 1990.

Rees, Richard. *Simone Weil: A Sketch for a Portrait*. Carbondale, IL: Southern Illinois University Press, 1966.

Weil, Simone. *Gravity and Grace*. London: Routledge, 2002.

———. "Letter 4: Spiritual Autobiography." In *Waiting for God*, 23–42. London: Routledge, 2021.

HUI'S FOURTH STORY: THE GREEN PLACE

Somerville, Madeleine. "How I Deal with the Unbearable Hypocrisy of Being an Environmentalist." *Guardian* (US edition), April 5, 2016. theguardian.com/lifeandstyle/2016/apr/05environmentally-friendly-green-living-ideas.

Sullivan, John. "'Greenwashing' Gets His Goat: Environmental Activist Coined Famous Term." *Times Herald-Record*, August 1, 2009. eu.recordonline.com/story/news/2009/08/01/greenwashing-gets-his-goat/51926672007.

Swain, Glenn. "On the Alert for Misleading Ads." *New York Times*, November 16, 2011. archive.nytimes.com/green.blogs.nytimes.com/2011/11/16/on-the-alert-for-misleading-ads.

Watson, Bruce. "The Troubling Evolution of Corporate Greenwashing." *Guardian* (US edition), August 20, 2016. theguardian.com/sustainable-business/2016/aug/20/greenwashing-environmentalism-lies-companies.

STORY FOUR AGAIN: THE GREEN PLACE

Bourdieu, Pierre. *Distinction: A Social Critique of the Judgement of Taste*. Translated by Richard Nice. London: Routledge, 2010.

HUI'S FIFTH STORY: THE TRUE WONDERS OF THE HOLY LAND

Agence France-Presse. "UN Doubles Estimate of Destroyed Gaza Homes." *Arab News*, December 19, 2014. arabnews.com/world/news/676536.

Amnesty International. "Israel's Apartheid Against Palestinians: A Look into Decades of Oppression and Domination." February 1, 2022. amnesty.org/en/latest/campaigns/2022/02/israels-system-of-apartheid.

Associated Press in Jerusalem. "Israeli-Palestinian Violence in 2014—Timeline." *Guardian* (US edition), November 18, 2014. theguardian.com/world/2014/nov/18/israel-palestinian-violence-timeline.

Berman, Lazar, and Ilan Ben Zion. "Temple Mount Activist Shot, Seriously Hurt Outside Jerusalem's Begin Center." *Times of Israel*, October 29,

2014. timesofisrael.com/man-shot-seriously-injured-outside-jerusalems-begin center.

Brand, Chad, Archie England, and Charles W. Draper, eds. *Holman Illustrated Bible Dictionary*. Nashville, TN: Holman Bible Publishers, 2003.

Defense for Children International Palestine. *Operation Protective Edge: A War Waged on Gaza's Children*. DCIP, April 16, 2015. dci-palestine.org/operation_protective_edge_a_war_waged_on_gaza_s_children_resource.

Eglash, Ruth, and Griff Witte. "Clashes in East Jerusalem after Teen's Burial Revive Intifada Fears for Middle East." *Washington Post*, July 5, 2014. washingtonpost.com/world/2014/07/05/a9f5c538-d2a8-463d-b5cb-ec5f4fa0ab37_story.html.

Erlanger, Steven. "In Gaza, Airstrikes and Economic Stress Make for an Anxious Ramadan." *New York Times*, July 11, 2014. nytimes.com/2014/07/12/world/middleeast/for-gazans-a-tense-and-somber-ramadan.html.

Khadder, Kareem, Samira Said, and Susanna Capelouto. "Palestinian Teen Burned Alive, Autopsy Shows." CNN, July 5, 2014. edition.cnn.com/2014/07/05/world/meast/mideast-tensions.

*Middle East Monitor*. "The Ancient Mosques of Gaza in Ruins: How Israel's War Endangered Palestine's Cultural Heritage." September 10, 2014. middleeastmonitor.com/20140910-the-ancient-mosques-of-gaza-in-ruins-how-israels-war-endangered-palestines-cultural-heritage.

Thrall, Nathan. "Rage in Jerusalem." *London Review of Books* 36, no. 23 (December 4, 2014): 19–21.

United Nations Office for the Coordination of Humanitarian Affairs, Occupied Palestinian Territory. *Fragmented Lives: Humanitarian Overview 2014*. OCHA oPt, March 2015. ochaopt.org/sites/default/files/Annual_Humanitarian_Overview_2014_English_final.pdf.

———. "Key Figures on the 2014 Hostilities." June 23, 2015. ochaopt.org/content/key-figures-2014-hostilities.

———. *Occupied Palestinian Territory: Gaza Emergency Situation Report (as of 4 September 2014, 08:00 hrs)*. OCHA oPt, September 2014. ochaopt.org/content/occupied-palestinian-territory-gaza-emergency-situation-report-4-september-2014-0800-hrs.

———. *Protection of Civilians: Reporting Period 28 October–3 November 2014*. OCHA oPt, December 2014. ochaopt.org/content/protection-civilians-weekly-report-28-october-3-november-2014.

United Nations Office of the High Commissioner for Human Rights. "Israel's 55-Year Occupation of Palestinian Territory is Apartheid—UN Human Rights Expert." OHCHR, March 25, 2022. ohchr.org/en/press-releases/2022/03/israels-55-year-occupation-palestinian-territory-apartheid-un-human-rights.

———. "UN Gaza Inquiry Finds Credible Allegations of War Crimes
Committed in 2014 by Both Israel and Palestinian Armed Groups."
OHCHR, June 22, 2015. ohchr.org/en/press-releases/2015/06/un-gaza-
inquiry-finds-credible-allegations-war-crimes-committed-2014-both.
United Nations Relief and Works Agency for Palestine Refugees in the
Near East. "2014 Gaza Conflict." Accessed November 26, 2023. unrwa.
org/2014-gaza-conflict.

### ROOM

Ragsdale, Catherine. "The Tree Is a Body." *The Nasiona*, December 26, 2019,
thenasiona.com/2019/12/26/the-tree-is-a-body.

### THE STORY OF BODY

*Channel News Asia*. "Number of Suicides among Those in Their 20s Highest
in Singapore." August 3, 2020. web.archive.org/web/20200823153139/
https://www.channelnewsasia.com/news/singapore/suicide-sos-
samaritans-singapore-youths-aged-20s-12985146.
Teng, Amelia. "Singapore Families Spent $1.4b on Private Tuition for Kids
Last Year." *Straits Times*, September 24, 2019. straitstimes.com/singapore/
education/families-spent-14b-on-private-tuition-for-kids-last-year-as-
parents-fork-out.

### A NOTE ON ITALICS

Barokka, Khairani. "The Case Against Italicizing 'Foreign' Words." *Catapult*,
Feburary 11, 2020. catapult.co/stories/column-the-case-against-italicizing-
foreign-words-khairani-barokka.

IVAN WEISS

**SHZE-HUI TJOA** is a writer from Singapore who lives in the UK. She is a nonfiction editor at *Sundog Lit*, and previously served as fiction editor of *Exposition Review*. Her work has been published in journals including *Colorado Review*, *Southeast Review*, and *So to Speak*, and has been listed as notable in three successive issues of *The Best American Essays* series (2021-23). Her work has received support from the Tin House Summer Workshop, the Vermont Studio Center, the Voices of Our Nations Arts Foundation, Disquiet International, and AWP's Writer to Writer Mentorship Program.